REHABILITATION OF THE DRUG ABUSER WITH DELINQUENT BEHAVIOR

Publication Number 896

AMERICAN LECTURE SERIES®

A Publication in
The BANNERSTONE DIVISION *of*

AMERICAN LECTURES IN SOCIAL AND REHABILITATION PSYCHOLOGY

Consulting Editors

JOHN G. CULL, Ph.D.

Director, Regional Counselor Training Program
Department of Rehabilitation Counseling
Virginia Commonwealth University
Fishersville, Virginia

and

RICHARD E. HARDY, Ed.D.

Chairman, Department of Rehabilitation Counseling
Virginia Commonwealth University
Richmond, Virginia

The American Lecture Series in Social and Rehabilitation Psychology offers books which are concerned with man's role in his milieu. Emphasis is placed on how this role can be made more effective in a time of social conflict and a deteriorating physical environment. The books are oriented toward descriptions of what future roles should be and are not concerned exclusively with the delineation and definition of contemporary behavior. Contributors are concerned to a considerable extent with prediction through the use of a functional view of man as opposed to a descriptive, anatomical point of view.

Books in this series are written mainly for the professional practitioner; however, academicians will find them of considerable value in both undergraduate and graduate courses in the helping services.

REHABILITATION OF THE DRUG ABUSER WITH DELINQUENT BEHAVIOR

Case Studies and Rehabilitation Approaches In Drug Abuse and Delinquency

RICHARD E. HARDY

JOHN G. CULL

CHARLES C THOMAS • PUBLISHER

Springfield • Illinois • U.S.A.

Published and Distributed Throughout the World by

CHARLES C THOMAS • PUBLISHER
Bannerstone House
301-327 East Lawrence Avenue, Springfield, Illinois, U.S.A.

ISBN 0-398-02823-0

Library of Congress Catalog Card Number: 73-216

With THOMAS BOOKS careful attention is given to all details of manufacturing and design. It is the Publisher's desire to present books that are satisfactory as to their physical qualities and artistic possibilities and appropriate for their particular use. THOMAS BOOKS will be true to those laws of quality that assure a good name and good will.

Printed in the United States of America
R-1

This book is dedicated
to our parents

Mr. and Mrs. Clifford E. Hardy

and

Mr. and Mrs. John G. Cull

PREFACE

REHABILITATION work with the drug abuser whose behavior has become delinquent is developing rapidly as a professional area of endeavor. No field is fraught with more problems for both the helpee and the helper. This book attempts to assess the current status, trends and problems through a case study approach as these relate to work of rehabilitation counselors, psychologists and others who are attempting to find their way toward offering improved services to this group.

Rehabilitation services broadly defined are in such great demand throughout the country especially in schools, colleges, community agencies and hospitals that every effort must be made in order to present knowledge in a meaningful manner. We have offered material in case study description form in order that the reader can rapidly get a feel for some of the types of problems, failures and successes that presently constitute the picture in the area of rehabilitation of persons who are experiencing difficulty in adjusting.

All persons need help from friends and associates at times, and it seems that most people are interested in philosophical concerns about the meaning and purpose of living. The mastery of one's environment is all important. Many of the persons described in this book have experienced serious difficulties in these areas.

The authors wish to thank the many individuals and organizations involved in allowing these materials to be developed. Of necessity, these organizations will remain anonymous. Special thanks go to William R. Crunk, Jr. who assisted in the preparation of some of the material.

RICHARD E. HARDY
JOHN G. CULL

CONTENTS

Page

Preface vii

Chapter

1. A Therapeutic Approach to the Rehabilitation of the Youthful Drug Abuser 3
2. Case Studies 13

Frank 15
R. C. A. 32
A. B. T. 42
M. J. J. 45
J. A. S. 52
L. B. J. 59
B. B. T. 64
H. P. D. 67
T. M. T. 72
C. W. B. 75
W. D. R. 81
R. E. M. 89
S. T. K. 96
R. G. L. 100
B. T. S. 107
D. A. L. 117
C. A. B. 119
C. L. C. 123
A. S. C. 126
J. G. S. 131
F. R. J. 140
D. L. L. 145
E. D. W. 150

Chapter *Page*

H. A. W. 155
P. A. R. 158
J. W. W. 165
G. A. L. 171
3. Language of the Drug Abuser 175

Index 195

REHABILITATION OF THE DRUG ABUSER WITH DELINQUENT BEHAVIOR

The following books have appeared thus far in this Series:

VOCATIONAL REHABILITATION: PROFESSION AND PROCESS
John G. Cull and Richard E. Hardy

CONTEMPORARY FIELD WORK PRACTICES IN REHABILITATION
John G. Cull and Craig R. Colvin

SOCIAL AND REHABILITATION SERVICES FOR THE BLIND
Richard E. Hardy and John G. Cull

FUNDAMENTALS OF CRIMINAL BEHAVIOR AND CORRECTIONAL SYSTEMS
John G. Cull and Richard E. Hardy

MEDICAL AND PSYCHOLOGICAL ASPECTS OF DISABILITY
A. Beatrix Cobb

DRUG DEPENDENCE AND REHABILITATION APPROACHES
Richard E. Hardy and John G. Cull

INTRODUCTION TO CORRECTIONAL REHABILITATION
Richard E. Hardy and John G. Cull

VOLUNTEERISM: AN EMERGING PROFESSION
John G. Cull and Richard E. Hardy

APPLIED VOLUNTEERISM IN COMMUNITY DEVELOPMENT
Richard E. Hardy and John G. Cull

VOCATIONAL EVALUATION FOR REHABILITATION SERVICES
Richard E. Hardy and John G. Cull

ADJUSTMENT TO WORK
John G. Cull and Richard E. Hardy

SPECIAL PROBLEMS IN REHABILITATION
A Beatrix Cobb

THE NEGLECTED OLDER AMERICAN
John G. Cull and Richard E. Hardy

Chapter I

A THERAPEUTIC APPROACH TO THE REHABILITATION OF THE YOUTHFUL DRUG ABUSER

- *Application Criteria*
- *Background of the Program Participants*
- *Service Delivery System*
- *Staffing and Training*
- *Impact and Results*
- *Summary*

APPROXIMATELY three years ago, the SEED was founded in Fort Lauderdale, Florida, by Art and Shelly Barker. The basic design of the program is the general treatment model developed by Alcoholics Anonymous; however, there are several modalities which are peculiar to the SEED. The description which follows is basically an outline of the goals and methods of the program; however, certain intangibles which are difficult to describe exist in the program.

The SEED was developed because of a desperate need for help which existed for young people in the Fort Lauderdale area as a result of the heightened incidence of drug abuse. It was felt that new approaches to the problem were needed; therefore, the SEED concept evolved. The SEED program's concept was based on the premise that man can change his behavior and can live and cope in his environment. The young people who seek help from the SEED program learn that they can no longer "cop out" with drugs; but that they have daily problems and must learn to live with them. At the SEED, they obtain a sense of belonging to something meaningful along with the knowledge that they can find purpose in their lives with the extra ingredient – a sense of dedication toward helping themselves and helping others to help themselves. The primary function of the SEED program is to provide rehabilitative services for the young person who has become a drug experimenter, user, abuser, or addict.

Application Criteria

The SEED is made available to anyone needing help. The addict who must have some sort of maintenance – such a Methadone – to assist him in achieving detoxification will not be accepted by the SEED until such time as he is able to tolerate a truly "cold turkey" program of abstinence. Since its main program is not detoxification, the aim is to work with the experimenter, user, abuser, or addict who has used drugs less than ten years. Because of the age range – nine years to early twenties – parental consent of the majority of applicants is needed.

Anyone seeking help from the SEED and in need of detoxification treatment is referred to the appropriate facilities. Those applicants who are in need of medical attention are referred to appropriate hospitals and/or their private physicians. These young people then come back to the SEED program once they are considered to be in sound medical health. Other than these selected criteria, the SEED makes no distinction concerning participation in the program.

Physical discomfort of "withdrawal" is at a minimum among participants. Even those young people who have used heroin for two or more years and have $200-a-day habits (this is equivalent to $60 to $65 in New York) take only approximately three days to pass through the withdrawal symptoms.

Background of the Program Participants

A unique factor of the SEED program is that it reaches into the schools. In this community, estimates show that between 70 and 85 percent of the children are experimenting with, using, or abusing drugs. The SEED has been successful in reaching young people through referrals made by principals, teachers, and counselors of the various schools in Broward County. The apparent change in students using drugs such as the decline of grades, failures, and dropouts, along with attitude change has added to the frustration and dilemma of educators. Due to the referrals made by educators to the SEED program, the majority of the young people destined to become delinquents and burdens on society have been able to continue in school education and to aid teachers in understanding the drug problems of the young. The young abuser is of considerable help in helping other drug abusers since he understands not only the values but also the language of the drug culture (Hardy and Cull, 1973).

Many young people, no matter how well they progress, have environmental backgrounds which are quite impossible for them in terms of adjustment. If there is no reinforcement from the family, the young person will meet constantly with disappointment and discouragement. For those young people in this particular situation, the SEED has been able to assist with the cooperation of either the courts and/or various agencies (vocational rehabilitation, family services, etc.) in obtaining foster homes and has been successful in continuing to work with them in their new environments.

Service Delivery System

The first phase of the SEED's program consists, in most cases, of a two-week program of intensive group discussions but is expandable when needed. During this two-week period, the group discussion sessions average approximately twelve hours per day. In these sessions, the participant is aided in gaining insight into what he is and what he has done to his life by taking drugs; but more importantly, he learns what his life can be for him and the impact he can have on others if he is *straight.* These two weeks represent the equivalent in time of the participant's going to a psychologist and/or psychiatrist for a period of three years on a one-hour, once-a-week basis. The 14-day intensive group sessions provide a radical and comprehensive change which facilitates the learning process of the participant. The SEED is operated on a continuous seven-day week basis. The participant in this 14-day program is at the SEED from 10 a.m. to 10 p.m., during which time he is involved constantly in "rap" sessions under the supervision of staff. These rap sessions are carefully guided and the intensity is maintained at a controlled, effective level. When necessary for certain individual needs, "rap" sessions also are held on a one-to-one basis with a staff member.

Upon successful completion of this first phase, an additional three-month period ensues which requires the participant to attend four group sessions a week. This phase of the program offers practical application of his learning processes. He learns to function and cope in his environment while returning to the group involvement. The criteria of success of this program are based not only on the fact that the young person is drug free, but also on his attitude change toward life; that is, there is a love of self and others, community and country, and a sense of dedication to help his fellow man.

Due to the age of participants, they can adjust well to change. The amount of attitude change in the individual seems to indicate that the three-month period is quite effective. In some instances, individuals require either an extension of the two-week period of an extension of the three-months' program. Periodic follow-up is done to see how the participants are doing.

If the participant learns well and grasps the meaning of honesty, love, respect, discipline, and affection, there is no need for him to go back to drugs. For the young people who are found to have deep-rooted psychological, or serious physical problems, the SEED makes referrals to medical doctors, psychologists, and/or other community programs. This is true particularly during the individual's participation in the two-week intensive program.

Up until his introduction to the SEED, the *druggie's* best, most reliable friend has been the lie that he speaks and lives in order to mislead his parents and his teachers. This same lie directed to a staff member at the SEED is guaranteed to trigger a *choicely worded* verbal barrage not soon to be forgotten. Why? Because the staff member is a former *druggie* himself and can *smell* a lie that you or I would accept as fact!

Because it is tough to lose an old friend – and the lie has been his *best* friend – it must be replaced with something of at least equal value. This is where the SEED asserts its true strength and individuality. Just after the above-described verbal barrage, the staff member will close the one-on-one session by saying to the thoroughly deflated recreant, "I love you." No one who has heard this shopworn phrase as it is spoken at the SEED can fail to be deeply moved by the sincerity and purpose behind its use. The reinforcing effect of true concern (love) is quite awesome.

The success of the SEED program also depends largely on family participation. The families are encouraged to attend two meetings a week to participate with the young people. Through this participation, the parents can get an overall picture of what the SEED is about and can see the gradual improvement of not only their own children but also those of other parents. They also can acquaint themselves with these other parents.

The group participation of parents and children, particularly those parents who are deeply involved with the program, has produced remarkable results in that the family unit is brought closer together and gains a better understanding of the dynamics of its problem. Also it has been observed that a greater level of love and compassion evolves within the family.

Fundamental to the continuing success of the SEED's program – especially during the period immediately following the two-week initial phase – is a highly effective intelligence network put together by Art Barker, which is composed of ex-druggies, teachers, police and concerned friends. If an apparently rehabilitated participant is seen even talking with an unreconstructed acquaintance, Art knows about it in a matter of minutes and is able to get to the offender for further therapy before recividism sets in.

Staffing and Training

The SEED has been able to train group leaders and help them develop talents of leadership. It also has been successful in encouraging these group leaders to continue more intensively in all endeavors to help combat the drug problem in the Fort Lauderdale area.

The SEED is strictly a paraprofessional organization with its group leaders and staff coming from the program. Because of its uniqueness, the quality of staffing can be maintained only on this basis. Art Barker is responsible for the overall operation of the program and for seeing that the outline and guidelines which have been developed are followed and the objectives fulfilled. He is also responsible for seeing that the other personnel maintain a high level of proficiency in meeting their obligations and fulfilling job requirements. Additionally, he is a liaison officer with other agencies in the community to effect cooperation and coordinate efforts that benefit the community maximally without duplicating existing services.

There are four senior group leaders whose responsibility it is to maintain group supervision when groups are in session. They assist in training new group leaders and junior group leaders. The junior group leaders are individuals who have gained some insight into the workings of the SEED program, but as yet have not developed the maturity or had experience which would perpare them to take a major responsibility for the conduct of either the initial intensive group sessions or the latter therapeutic group sessions. As they gain responsibility, they move on to being senior group leaders and assume a role of deeper responsibility. The staff of the SEED program, 25 paid and 15 volunteers, can effectively handle the approximately three hundred active participants in the program.

Impact and Results

The SEED has had a demonstrable impact in the Fort Lauderdale area. Its program has reached into the courts, the jails, the minority ghetto areas, and the schools of Broward County. The Broward County Personnel Association officially has adopted the SEED as its 1971 drug project and is assisting in obtaining employment for the successful young people while in, as well as when leaving the SEED program. The district supervisor of the Florida Parole and Probation Office and his staff have been playing a vital role in the rehabilitation of these people during and after their participation in the SEED program. The SEED also uses resources such as Broward General Hospital, Henderson Clinic, Family Services, Community Services, Vocational Rehabilitation, and adult education on an emergency and a referral basis. The SEED recently became a member of the Cooperative Area Manpower Planning System (CAMPS) which is sponsored by the local city governments of Fort Lauderdale and Broward County. CAMPS is attempting to create a force of local agencies to effectively coordinate and cooperate in employment-developing opportunities. One role of the SEED is that of rehabilitating young people to enable them to become employable and constructive members of society and their community; therefore, involvement with these other social action agencies is essential.

It is interesting that the professionals who visit the SEED to observe the program seem to elevate different factors to prominence. One man might be struck by the obvious affection which permeates relationships between staff and participants; another by the sense of discipline displayed; and a third by the basic honesty of the program.

We feel the most effective factor influencing the youthful drug abuser at the SEED is peer pressure. The youthful ex-drugee is a potent influence in exerting conformity behavior. Cull (1971) has shown that peer pressure is influencial even among schizophrenics who have rejected interaction with the social world in a manner somewhat similar to the members of the drug culture. Social roles are changing rapidly. No longer do the elders in our culture exert the impact on behavior and judgments they did in the past (Cull, 1970); consequently, the SEED has turned to the group which can exert sufficient social pressure to change behavior – the youthful *ex-drugees.*

The drug dependence problem is one of the most pressing in the country, and Broward County is no exception. This is evidenced primarily by arrests, particularly of the youth between ages 13 and 20. The SEED's records substantiate this age span and document the fact that many youths start on drugs at an early age and advance from marijuana to hard narcotics within one year. In an effort to combat the drug problem, the SEED was founded approximately two years ago. The basic model for the program is the general treatment program developed by Alcoholics Anonymous, with some very important modifications.

The counselors or staff members are rehabilitated drug

offenders. After having gone through the program themselves, they have been judged to have the necessary skills and motivations to assist in helping others. These skills consist basically of the ability to develop an empathic relationship with others, the presence of strong desires and a dedication to help others and themselves, and finally, the ability to become skillful and successful group leaders.

The group sessions may be categorized loosely with the more formal Guided Group Interaction and Transactional Analysis type groups. In the sessions of the SEED, both formal and informal group pressures are brought to bear upon the individual members by other members and leaders. As may be expected, it takes a very skillful leader to know when and how to apply pressure to any particular member or any particular segment of the group. This leader also must know how to channel the group's pressures to effective and fruitful endeavors. The group leaders are extremely adept at reading the character of each member and then applying or halting the pressures. Having once been drug offenders themselves, they are able to pierce the protective shell which each drug offender throws about himself. The group leaders refuse to fall into the verbal and the cognitive traps which the drug offender erects. In the language of Transactional Analysis, the leaders see the games drug abusers may be playing and refuse to play them. They then point out to the individual how false ideas have led him to his present state of affairs.

The atmosphere where this guided group interaction takes place contains simply *affection, empathy, discipline,* and *love.* This *love* is a powerful tool in the hands of skilled leaders. In social power terms, the leader has been endowed referent power by the other members of the group. While at no time will he deny any group member, he does, however, skillfully manage the application of power. He uses his power to maintain motivation by reassuring those members who may have just received the brunt of a group session.

The above-described atmosphere of love has been coupled with the skillful handling of guided group interactions to form the SEED's unique and highly successful program. A new member attends two full weeks of twelve-hour sessions. If he has not made adequate progress, he may continue for two more weeks. Once a member has shown that he is responding, he is then allowed to return home. Prior to this he has stayed in the home of another participant and has gone to school or work from that home. After finishing this period, he returns to SEED for further group sessions every night for three hours and all day Saturday. This process lasts for three months. The member is then *straight* and attends only once or twice a week from then on.

During the day, there are two separate groups – one for males, the other for females. Particular problems are discussed and solutions found. In the evening, there is a general session which every member attends. The staff members take turns leading the discussion and help each other whenever necessary. Twice a week there is an open session in which parents, friends, teachers, probation and parole officers, and concerned others participate. At the open meetings, there are usually about 250 members and up to 400 visitors.

An essential element in the success of the SEED is the amount of community participation and aid. Referrals to the SEED program come through many channels. Some are self-referrals, others come because of parental or peer pressure. The various courts are probating individuals to the SEED and sometimes send an individual to it for a pre-sentence diagnostic type study. Many individuals, of course, come because of the attention of concerned adults such as relatives, teachers and police officials. The SEED, because of its unique method and unequaled success ratio (now claimed to be over 90 percent), has managed to gather full community support.

Summary

In summary, the SEED is an organization of former drug offenders who are dedicated to helping others. Its program of guided group interaction, honesty, concern, and understanding seems to have meshed into a workable method. The testimony of parents, doctors, friends, teachers, prison officials, members of school boards, and others all point to the fact that the SEED is a viable, dynamic program.

REFERENCES

Berne, Eric: Transactional Analysis in Psychotherapy. New York, Grove Press, 1961.

Cull, J. G.: Age as a factor in achieving conformity behavior, Journal of Industrial Gerontology. Spring, 1970.

Cull, J. G.: Conformity behavior in schizophrenics, Journal of Social Psychology. Vol. 117, July 1971.

Hardy, R. E. and Cull, J. G.: Language of the drug abuser. In Hardy, R. E., Cull, J. G., Drug Dependence and Rehabilitation. Springfield, Thomas, 1973.

Urbanik, Richard: Report on the SEED: a working drug treatment program in Fort Lauderdale, Florida, Department of Correction, State of North Carolina, 1971 (unpublished).

Chapter 2

CASE STUDIES

Case Study 1

FRANK

My name is Frank and I was born in the Bronx. I lived there the first fourteen years of my life and then we moved to New Jersey. My family consisted of my mother and father and two older brothers. We were not starving. We were pretty well off. It was normal, nothing upper or middle class, but we were doing pretty well; however, I would say at this time financially things were getting a little worse. We owned a home in the Bronx and the reason for moving was to get to a better environment and it was a suburb in New Jersey that promised this. But, also, the finances, to keep the house that we had in the Bronx, just were not there any more so we moved in with an aunt in New Jersey.

I attended high school. Before that I went to Catholic schools. I went to public school in New Jersey, my grades dropped sharply. My motivation, I imagined, seemed to have come from other people. You know, always pushing in Catholic school. I did well in Catholic school but, as I said, in public high school my grades really went down. I just made it through the first three years and I think the last year of high school was sort of a gift from the school to me. When I came out of school I didn't have any sort of goals or any ambition to accomplish a set thing. I just sort of drifted around. I turned my part time job in a delicatessen and at a supermarket into a full time job and really the only thing that I worked for was I wanted to purchase a motorcycle. I was 17 or 18 years old then and I went to beauty school to be a hair dresser. I did not do much with that and the following September, after being out of high school a year and a half, I went to men's barbering school. I really still, as of that time, only accomplished buying a motorcycle.

In barber school which was in New York City, again we were still living in New Jersey, I was first as you could say introduced to drugs other than just knowing of people who "did" them in high school. In New York City I actually saw at this time people using drugs. I was 18 years old then and there were other fellows in the school using drugs. My involvement or first time use was in

Newark, New Jersey, when I went for a draft physical for induction into the service. It was the pre-physical before you go in – like a couple of months before. I ran into a friend who I had known a year or so before who I knew did some drugs. He told me about heroin, that was the drug he was using. Things were not looking really lousy for me but they were, you know, as usual running along on the same scale. He talked to me about heroin, offered me some and there was no reason not to "do it." I knew some of the effects on the majority of the people I knew who had done heroin – it would never happen to me. So that afternoon I tried heroin. He mainlined me – he hit me – he cooked it up and he shot it into my vein and I liked the feeling. For the next six months, with this fellow primarily, I did drugs – heroin. I smoked marijuana about three or four times, but the drug we did was heroin. I was not physically addicted although I was getting to where I was doing it as often as I could obtain it which would be sometimes as much as three or four days a week, sometimes two times during the day.

This went on, like I said, for six months until February 1966 when I was drafted into the army. I had a choice then to either stop drugs or go into the service. My record was clean. I had not been arrested for anything. The money obtained to use drugs prior to this was mostly by selling a small amount of drugs to other people and shoplifting. I went into the service mostly because I just did not want to get a record and say that I was a drug addict to anybody. My family knew a little bit about it. Maybe they would notice that I was stoned sometimes and that there was no smell of alcohol on my breath but there was no big thing made out of it. I was not any worse than I was in the past and I had not shown much to them lately so they did not make a big thing of it. They knew that I would have to go into the service and maybe this would help me.

I went into the service and cleaned up for a few days in basic training at Fort Dix. There were drugs down there – marijuana primarily. I then wanted to get some heroin, I wanted to get out. I did not like the service but there was no way I could get any drug down there it seemed. I really did not have enough motivation to leave – to split the service. I wanted to get out on a medical discharge. I was going to shoot heroin, in basic, and they would catch me sooner or later and then get put out on a medical, I figured. I wasn't going to do any war and everything else, or bring any other complication into it. But, nobody would bring any drug down to me and by the time I got a day home from the service I had been in about six weeks and I was starting to feel good. I had gained a lot of weight and physically I felt good and mentally I was accomplishing something. I was starting to think a little bit, even if it is just the level that they let you think in the army, but I was starting to accomplish something. I was doing well in basic training, nothing fantastic but I was doing better than I ever did before in my life in competition, and I liked it. I liked the way I felt. I went home on leave before I went down to Oklahoma and I did not touch drugs. I went to Oklahoma for a tour of training. I stayed there. There we smoked on a few occasions. Other friends were doing heavier drugs. I really just could not get a good connection with someone I could trust and they were arresting people for drugs, so I just didn't want to get in trouble.

From there I went directly to Germany, to Neuremburg. During my stay in Germany there was hash over there. There were drugs over there. I wasn't involved with people using them and thus I myself did not get involved. I did not go looking for them. I stayed clean all the time I was over there. Although over there as a soldier I started to deteriorate. I was late for formations and I was not as sharp as I should have been. I just about stayed out of trouble and just made it away from getting an Article 15 on quite a few occasions. I spent almost nine months in Germany. During that time 1049th, volunteered to go to Viet Nam. The 1049th came through. I was granted permission to go to Viet Nam. I went home for 50 days on a leave, again came in contact with drugs a few times but did not use any drugs. I had been engaged to a girl before I went over. At this time I broke the engagement and I went over there just to fight this war that they talked about. Well I got there and within two to three days I was smoking pot. Drugs were just all over the place in Viet Nam, everywhere. As soon as I hit my unit, the first night there, some fellows came and asked me if I would like to come out to the bunker. I came out and they were passing a joint around and it was just accepted that you know they figured that I would smoke. I do not know how they got the idea that I had used drugs. I did not tell anyone. All I said was where I was from. I know everyone there from the East Coast smoked. So I smoked pot in Viet Nam chronically. We smoked continuously. There is another word that describes it. When we woke up in the morning I would smoke pot until I went to bed at night, just about every occasion we could. I worked a lot of times on the night shift. I was in "play cool" with the artillary. I was in fire direction control. So I would work night shift sometimes and then day shift for awhile. But when I was on night shift I would stay stoned. It was the same with the day shift. I was in a combat unit with artillery. We saw combat quite a number of times and it did not seem to phase anyone. It was you know nothing was said you were smoking pot because you might die tomorrow. It was that you just did not give-a-care type of attitude. Altogether I think that made it so rampant over there plus the drugs were readily available and really inexpensive. We would purchase a pack of marijuana, already rolled, twenty cigarettes in American paper filtered for $3, that was the most you paid. The only drug I did while over there though was marijuana. There were other drugs. No one else I knew in our unit, except a medic, was doing anything else except for a little bit of smoking opium. But, the majority of drug use in our unit was marijuana. This was 1967 and at the very beginning of 1968, I left there in February.

I came back to the U. S. and I really was not looking for drugs, I was happy to be home, glad to be alive. While over there I had done well, I won a bronze star in combat. I came home ready for civilian life expecting things to be a lot different. I was a bit different from when I went over there. I was a bit stoned also I would say. I did not bring any drugs back and I was not looking for any, as I said. But, a friend picked me up, the first buddy I ran into since I was back, and he offered me a joint. He was just coming out of the Navy and he and I were talking about overseas and things. Before we knew it it was drugs. He knew I used to shoot dope a few years before. He never did and he offered me some pot and we started smoking. Within a month I would say, I started going and copping dope, marijuana, and copping some quantity of it and reselling it. I would get a couple ounces of pot and break it down to $5 bags, you know nickle bags, and sell them to friends. I was falling back into the same thing.

My family said I deserved a vacation and so did I. I tried to get unemployment and I couldn't, it would take me 6 months to get unemployment. I came out and did drugs – marijuana. I was selling the marijuana and people were buying it and it was a good business. I had a few thousand dollars saved up from the service. I went on vacations down to Florida, I flew out to California. I traveled around quite a bit and I stayed stoned constantly, mostly just smoking pot and drinking wine. This went on for a few months and people asked about other drugs if I could get them. Other people were doing other drugs. I got some acid and before I sold it I did it and I started tripping maybe once a week. Then I was selling ups and downs, mostly seconals and tuminals and stuff like diet pills, different types of amphetamines. I did a few of the ups but mostly I liked the down pills. Within that first six month that I was out I was doing quite a bit of downs. After being out six months I must have been doing about 5 or 10 a day along with smoking pot and little bit of drinking. The drinking was starting to die down. This kept up a little while and then at nine months it got up to 10. Ten was what I was always doing a day and more.

Our family was living in a different town. We had our own place. Both my brothers were married and out of the house. I was the only one there. People were making all sorts of excuses, you know the war did it to him, drugs are doing it to him and nobody wants to help him. People sort of left me alone. I hadn't had any problem with the police until just about this time which was late 1968. I had been out of the service almost a year. I was selling an awful lot of drugs. I was going out to California now and buying kilos of pot and bringing them back. Then I stopped doing the transporting and a friend in Brooklyn, New York, was doing it. I was buying it from him at quite a bit more money but it was a lot safer. I was selling weight in drugs. I was selling quantity of marijuana, quantity of acid, quantity of pills to other fellows who were then dealing. I was making quite a bit of money too. There were times when I was taking off for drugs. There were times when I was beat – which means bought bad drugs. But, I always seemed to come back out of the hole, there was always somebody who would front some money to me and I would be able to do a transaction, do some business. To me it was a business but also it was staying stoned. It was a way of life I guess.

Near the end of that first year home, well after the first 9 months home, the police were pretty much on to me and I had to watch myself then. I lived at a few different friend's places. I had to leave the state a couple of times and still try to carry on my transactions of selling drugs from out of state or from different houses. Mostly I was then just selling quantity and other people were doing it for me. A couple of them got busted. A few times my name was given out, the police were hot on me but usually I was able to make it away. I then moved into an apartment and sort of set up shop. I started really dealing pretty heavily now. I was doing around 15 downs a day now. These were the nembutals which we were getting right from the factory, and at a fantastic price. I was pretty messed up on them. I started popping them as soon as I got up right until I fell out at night. I was not sleeping too much. I had lost all sorts of weight. I was smoking pot constantly. Every friend I knew was a drug user. My house was a sort of meeting place and a buying place, a trading place. It became quite a scene. We were tripping every week and doing just about any drug imaginable but I had not gone back to heroin. I said I was not a drug addict as long as I was not doing heroin. I was not a junkie. I was not beating anybody really. I was selling people drugs, they wanted them and there is nothing wrong with that, just because it is illegal. The establishment doesn't know what it is talking about. There is nothing wrong with drug use. I am not stealing from anybody and I did not feel like I was doing anything wrong. This went on for a few months until February 1969. At that time my name was given to the police in town that morning or something and they put a warrant right out that I had been known in the county. The county police came to the apartment, broke in, caught a number of people at the house and found a large quantity of drugs. I had sold quite a bit but they still found about five pounds of marijuana, a number of tabs of acid, about 25. They found needles and other kinds of works. I kept my downs in a milk bottle in my drawer and they found all of those and assorted pills. They hit me with a disorderly house, under the influence and possession of marijuana. Everyone else in the house was given the same charges of possession and influence.

We went to preliminary court three times and everybody else was dropped loose and mine was sent to the Grand Jury. So figured there I have a wait. I cut my hair and I got a job. At the time I had long hair and a full beard. I cleaned up and got a job so that it would look good for court. I was pretty down and out about being busted. I had stopped dealing drugs. I had money to live on. When I got the job I was living on that. It was strange because I wanted to stop associating with so many of these people because I knew I was hot and the police were watching me. In turn a few people came to me for downs. A couple of these people were junkies, they were drug addicts, heroin addicts. They still came around for the downs because I seemed to still have them, my own supply. I said "no, I am not selling any more."

One fellow was going over to the city to buy heroin in New York. I just went with him one day. I wanted to go and we bought a half load of dope, of heroin that is 15 bags. I paid for it and I think I gave him a couple of bags for taking me over and turning me on to the connection. I shot one bag of dope at that time and it would really get me high, really stoned. Then I started copping there and up in the Bronx, bags of dope, but within a month or so I was shooting it every day.

At the beginning I just shot it on the weekends and a couple of nights during the week. But, then it became every day, then in the morning and within a month I was getting off at least once a day. The next month it must have been a few times a day and I was starting to get a physical habit. I am pretty sure about that. I was starting to sell heroin. It was strange I went through the whole progression. I started with heroin without a progression and then cleaned up and did the normal progression most people go through but once I went back to heroin I went all out. I used a lot of dope at this time, quite a number of bags. I quickly went up to about 10 or 15 a day. These were two dollar bags that you buy in New

York and it was fairly decent dope at this time. This was 1969, as I said, beginning of 1969.

I was waiting trial in that case and I was shooting dope and selling dope. People would give me their money and I'd go buy dope. They would give me a certain amount of bags for it or else I would buy the drug for $2 and sell it for 3 or 4 dollars a bag. I would also take some dope out of each bag, so I was making out pretty well whenever I could get these sales going, and that was all the time. There were times when I went to New York two times, three times a day, in the middle of the night, early in the morning it did not make much difference. This went on for a few months.

I was starting to get some enemies because some people would give me their money and I would just take all the money. I started selling people bad dope, beating people by taking too much out of the bags and by just taking dope. My game was not stealing. I was not breaking into houses and things like this. There were a few checks here and there maybe that I wrote to make money but the majority of it was just hustling people, talking people out of their money. I seemed to be doing pretty well at it. At that time I was shooting about 25 bags a day. The highest I ever went up to was maybe two of these half loads, 30 bags of dope but that was not that often where I was able to hustle that much money up. Usually I would shoot 20-25 bags of dope and this went on for a few months there where I fluctuated back and forth.

I did this all summer and then in October I was arrested for needle and syringe and cooker which was "narcotic paraphernalia." I went through a red traffic light after just selling some stuff and was clean except for the syringe works. The cops went to pull me over for that and I threw the needle out. They picked me up. That is a misdemeanor in New Jersey so you do not go to grand jury with it. That is taken care of on a town level.

Before I went to court I went to Burgenpines Hospital to detoxify. I figured this would look good for court. I went there and at this time at Burgenpines all they had was a psychiatric ward on the 9th floor where they had everybody and anybody and this is where drug addicts wound up. There was no medication other than sleeping pills. I only got two or three of those at the time I was there. All they really did was give you a place to stay while you were kicking drugs and what they called under medical supervision. The majority of times there were two or three nurses up there and they really were not doing too much supervising. It was sort of free for all. The only reason I stayed was because of court. It was a lock up you could not get out, could not get many visitors except the immediate family. Nobody was really getting a high in there or anything with the medication they had in the place but it did not offer anything and it sort of turned me off. It is sad that some drug addicts go for help and this is the place where he might be sent first off. They get a bad taste of what help is like and do not come back. I know this is what happened to me, because after I went there the lawyer I had spoke to me about other rehabilitation and I said "no way, not after that place" because it was a crazy house. That is the word I used then and still use for it now. There was no medication you went through the withdrawal. Even though after two days on the street on my own, I really went there just for looks, the day I got out I shot dope. I went back to shooting dope just as I had before. I was selling just as much and quickly. I was clean only nine days, seven days there and two days before so my habit built up pretty quickly again. I had not gained any weight or start to look any better really. I got worse and worse, shooting dope and avoiding the police.

My family was really hot on me now. I was back home. They were hassling me. My girlfriend was expecting a baby. The weight seemed to be coming down. I was not working. I was just hustling constantly and I did not care what anyone thought. My mother and father were letting me stay home. They were• blaming everyone under the sun except me it seemed, and I loved it and I stayed there and shot dope. Then when my mother would find something in the house she might throw it out and that was it. No real hassle other than this court case coming up that I was talking about. In December I contracted serum hepatitis from a friend. I was not looking too well when I went to court. I told the lawyer that I had stopped and he talked to the judge, talked to him about my military record and my family.

The girl had the baby. I married her right after the baby was born. I thought this would help me clean up. I tried a methadone program just before court so they would see that I tried something. This is where you went in the morning and they give you a prescription for four tablets which were supposed to set you straight. I was still sick. I took the 4 tablets but I would still be sick for dope and I would shoot dope at night usually, and do the tablets in the morning. After a day and a half of that I did the pills two mornings and I just went and got the prescriptions but did not use the pills, I just kept shooting dope. Then you are supposed to go to a group therapy at night. I made two of those out of the week I was there. Then I just did not go back.

So when I went to court I had a lot of things on my side. I had just gotten a job but quit it two days before court but did not tell anybody. It was interferring with my going to New York and buying drugs and selling drugs. I was not making enough money there to justify giving up the business with the drugs so I stopped it. I was shooting about 20 bags of dope then or about $40 worth a day I would say. Sometimes it was not those kinds. I would buy $5 in Jersey, $7 bags in Jersey so I was shooting 15 or 20 bags of dope a day, between $30 and $40. I went to court and was given a suspended 5 year sentence, placed on probation for 3 years and fined $500.

I went across to the probation department that day to meet my officer. I told him it was just a marijuana bust. I told him I was just a pot head. He did not believe it. He said I did not look like a pot head. I was yellow from hepatitis, I was all drawn out, black rings around my eyes, etc. I looked like a dope fiend I guess. He checked my arms and I had tracks on both arms. He said he wanted me to come in for urine testing every week. I said "o.k." He told me no use drying out now I am going to give you a urine test when you come back. I said "fine." For a day and a half I tried to stay straight. Again it did not work. That Sunday before I was supposed to go see him, I saw him first on Friday, I was supposed to go back on Monday, I got high and when I came in I told him. I said "now you have got to try and help me somehow." He gave me the urine test and he told me to get straight. He wanted to see me again Wednesday. I came back Wednesday and there were fresh marks on my arm again. He wanted to see me Friday. I came back Friday, again fresh marks. The next week he had me come in Monday and Wednesday again, but then he had me come in Thursday, Friday and then it was an every day thing – five days a week. This went on for another couple of weeks. This was all of March. At the end of the month one night he had given me a couple of warnings if I did not get straight and get a job he would have to put me in jail. One night I went in there for a urine test and I filled the cup with water. He caught me after I had handed it in. He said it was cold and he brought me back in and told me he was going to have to put me in jail. I figured o.k. that is it. What can I do. I guess he thought I was married and had a child having been on probation a month and he asked me if I wanted to go into rehabilitation, if I wanted some help. I said "sure" you know I figured to myself anything is better than going across the street to the county jail. I had spent a few nights in jail and I figured the county jail would not be any better than those places.

I was right but he gave me an opportunity to go to Daytop Village in New York. He gave me a week to get into Daytop Village. That week I stayed straight all the way up to the second to the last day. I tried to get some dope. I got a bag of dope and snorted half of it. My wife found the other half and threw it out. I was fairly sick all that week, but I wanted not to go to jail, primarily. I wanted to get into this place and give it a try. So we went to Daytop Village the next week. I was accepted to come down for an interview. I waited around about 4 or 5 hours. They interviewed me and accepted me. The only reason I was there, I can say, was not to go to jail and to get the pressure off of me from my family. Everybody was happy that I was going to go into this rehabilitation center which was a therapeutic community; but as I said before just to stay out of jail. I imagine that is not enough motivation to stay because I only lasted 10 days. It was hard to stay those ten days. They had group sessions there and I just did not open up. I did not give anything, and one morning I split from Daytop Village.

I went back to New Jersey and I did not go to my family or anything. I went to some friends and that night I got high. That night as a matter of fact I fell out. Other times I had "ODed" on the street. This time I just went out and my friends stayed with me and kept me revived a bit. The rest of the seven days I spent on the street. I just stayed copping dope for people. I did not have any money. I went home a few times and stole money out of the house. I took some money from some people I knew out there and for seven days I just went back and forth to the city getting drugs. I was in New Jersey after I had been out, as I said, a week. This officer who knew me and had been speaking to my mother that week since she said I had split (he knew of me and helped me as a matter of fact before when I was using drugs and tried to talk to me and help me) picked me up, brought me to my probation officer and told the officer that I gave myself up. He put in a good word for me, I guess, and the probation officer rapped with me for about a minute or two that day. He said "I see you are back." "Look, Frank, all I can do is put you in jail, you will have to go to court and we will see what happens then." So I went over to the Bergen County Jail and I sat there for awhile. I figured everyone had given up on me and I was pretty down and out. I contemplated a lot of things just like I imagine everyone else does when they go to jail. You think of killing yourself or just forgetting about the people on the outside, not writing them or answering them or taking any visits. Then you say well now I got myself here and I will just stay here and do my time and get out and get high. I went through all that and then my family came to visit me. I talked with them. My wife just asked me what I was going to do. I said I wanted to stop shooting dope. I had seen what it had done to me now. I still was saying what the drugs had done to me. I never was blaming it on myself, but I realized that the position I was in I did not want to be in anymore, and for that reason alone I wanted to get some help. I did not want to stay in jail. I wanted to get into another rehabilitation center. I talked with her about it. I talked with my mother, my probation officer and the public defender I had for a lawyer at that time. The officer gave a good report, the probation officer, the policeman who arrested me, as I said, and said that I gave myself up and my family was pulling for me. When I went to court the judge gave me another opportunity. He sent me to Dismus House for drug addiction in Patterson, New Jersey. He told me to stay in there until I am released. He placed me on three years probation again and he kept the suspended 5 year sentence over my head in case I left I would have to go down to prison. I got to Dismus House about a week or 4 days later. I had spent 30-35 days in jail. This was May 6, 1970.

I went to Dismus House with the idea that I was home safe again, but this time I would be a little smarter and I would stay in this place instead of staying in jail. I had this attitude although I tried to tell the people there that I wanted to help myself. But, this was the attitude I really said that I had. I kept this attitude until I found out that all the other guys there or a large majority of them were trying to help themselves. Maybe everybody was not sure why they were helping themselves, why they wanted to stop doing drugs but they realized that drugs were a problem and they were with me. I knew doing drugs was not normal. Something was wrong with it, and if I wanted to keep doing drugs I would keep winding up in institutions. I would lose my family and would lose myself. When I started realizing this I started to say well as long as I am here I might as well try. Then it became as long as I am here I may as well do something. The fellows there were real and it started to become my way of life. I started to be truthful with myself and with other people. I started to talk about myself. I started to be concerned about myself, about the guys that were in there with me. We were all drug users helping each other. There were two clinical psychologists on the staff. Father Greco is the director. It became my home and it became a lot to me that I had not had before. People there worried about me and even more so I started to worry about people. The program offered group therapy, individual therapy, work therapy and education, in a community living. I would say that I would go along with the philosophy of treatment. It helped me, it has helped a lot of people over the years. They have been there about eight years. I think it is the way for a lot of dope fiends to get themselves together. I can not say that it is the way for everybody because it does not help everybody that goes in there. But, it is the way for some people, and if it can reach some people it definitely should stay in existence. I stayed there 13 1/2 months. During that time I worked on many different problems that I had and I helped other people, I can say that. It is a self-help program. It is a program that wants you to come in – you fucked yourself up – you get yourself back together and then you get out and go back on the street. I worked my way up from working on the newspaper baling machine and garbage collector to a supervisor in the program.

After 13 1/2 months, through the help of Father Greco, I was able to get a job in Delaware as a resident director of a drug program that just opened up down here. We follow Dismus' type of treatment. I got back with my wife and child and came down to Delaware and worked to help start this program. For awhile I was the only employee and mostly I just went around and sort of introduced the program. In the program here we use group therapy, encounter groups, reality groups, sensitivity groups – it is all wrapped up in one here. It is a group where the fellows can air their frustrations and their anxieties against each other and talk about things that are bothering them or have bothered them in the past, and mostly talk about what we are doing now and what we are going to do in the future. There is an individual therapist, clinical psychologist and a staff of intern psychologists. There is community living. The fellows all live together in a home style atmosphere, upstairs enlarged bedrooms, eat together and work together. There is work therapy, as I said – maintenance of the house, cooking of the meals, cleaning up, and we are going to get vocational training into the program. There is education. Any resident who has not finished high school will go on to secure a General Equivalency Diploma or if he is young enough just continue his education and go back to high school when he gets out. We handle people here which is different in business. We handle people here who have done any drug other than been physically addicted to opiates for a long period of time. Also there is an age limit of 16-25, and it is all male. The program consists of two different phases. Phase one where a resident lives here in the program 24 hours a day and gets visits and letters from his immediate family and that is it for four to six months. During that four to six months he works here as I said then he is evaluated by the staff. After that time he would go into phase two which is a re-entry phase. It is run sort of like a halfway house. The resident lives here, has therapy here and works or schools on the outside.

At this time he starts to earn his privileges back. He can start growing his hair. At the beginning he gets his hair cut short. He can start wearing any type of clothing he wants. There are restrictions on clothing in the first phase of the program. He can receive mail from people other than his family, get visits, phone calls, etc. During the first part of the program there is none of that and all of the mail that does come and go is censored.

We opened on September 1, took in our first residents during that month, and we now have two residents and a re-entry. I am pleased with the program, pleased with the staff we have here; and, I am happy to say things are working out and they are working out much better than I thought they would. Myself, I go to school at night. I would like to go and complete college. Vocation wise, I would like to stay in this type of work right now, counseling, and stay as resident director. I enjoy the counseling, working with the fellows, working in group therapy, working with them as a paraprofessional and rapping with them individually. I also enjoy, as resident director, running the house, the daily things that go on in the house, appointments that have to be made, food that has to be bought, repairs that have to be made and supplies other than food. I enjoy that. I enjoy working and going down to the prison, interviewing people and trying to help some other guys that are down there and get them up here or get them into another program. I am involved in other things going on, drug wise, in the state. I work on a drug evaluation team which evaluates people who are trying to get into any state drug program.

I am back with my wife and our son is with us. We live right at the program. The marriage has had its ups and downs just as anyone elses has, but the biggest thing I have learned is that everyones does and mine is nothing different, and there is no reason to give up because there are problems. My wife has learned that too, and things are pretty fine with that. Still I have times when I feel like getting high, times when I feel like giving up. I am sure everyone that is in this life gets those times. Maybe not getting high on dope but everyone has a cop out I could say that they think about taking. I just take it one day at a time, one problem at a time. I find that if I take too much on I then lose. You see I can handle just so much and it is funny the way the problems come down if I take them one at a time and get them taken care of completely. By the time the next one comes I am ready for it. Maybe I am just lucky, but that is the way that it has been going and I do not think it is going to get that bad where I can not handle it. I am happy with myself which is pretty good. I think it helps keep me straight. I am happy with what I am doing and with my family. I think this plays a large part for the recovered drug addict, a large part in staying clean. Too many fellows I think might have good intentions, come out and hit many obstacles. People do not want to hire us because of our records. The majority of drug users have a criminal record. People do not want to hire us because of our work backgrounds. How many drug addicts really have had work experience other than the programs they have worked in. As I said I have been lucky I stepped into something pretty good. I am working hard as hell to keep it and to be better at it. I am also hoping to work at helping the other drug addicts, the dope fiends like myself who might have it a little harder. I think for the drug problem to be really taken care of, all of society has to pitch in. It is a drug culture we live in. Drugs are everywhere, every day, all walks of life are exposed to them from aspirins, tv set talks about them, and advertisements. It is a hell of a battle we have got but we have to attempt to do something about it. As far as the recovered drug user goes if people would give them a chance, I think a lot of the times he would come up good. Many fellows go back to drugs for other reasons which I do not think anyone knows about. I know when I get that feeling to get high I can not give you a reason exactly why I stay straight except that I want to stay straight. I am sure that when other guys fall it is not because they wanted to hurt anybody or that they want to just end everything and go back to leading a life of crime or whatever, but it is just something that comes over you and it is pretty hard to handle. When you have done it so many years, a year of being straight or two years being straight at times is not enough. I think a lot of work is needed, a lot of research is needed as to why people get high in the first place and why they get high again. Why would someone get high after being through all I have been through or else someone else has been through. These are the things I am interested in right now. As I stated before, the drug program that I went through and that I work in is not the answer for everybody. I think that outpatient clinics are needed, residential treatment centers are needed. Methadone might be needed for some cases or to form some type of union with people. Detoxification centers are needed and trained staff, trained personnel, both paraprofessional and professional, are needed in all these centers. As I said here we have myself, an ex-drug user and a few other ex-drug users on the staff, trained psychologists and interns working together to combat the problem, to help the guys here realize what they are doing to themselves and what they can do for themselves. The drug scene today, I talk with people who are in it, has not changed all that much. Names are different, prices are different, quality of some of the drugs are different but it really is not as different as it used to be. From what I can gather it is the same – everyone is doing it, why not do it. There are so many frustrations out there. It is a way out. Older people used drugs, alcohol so why should not we, is what the younger people are saying. I can not really open up any one's eyes on that aspect of it except that it seems everything is geared toward drugs and pleasure and so it is hard to say to the young people do not use them. As I said before everybody has their cop out.

Future wise I will continue with my education, continue with my job here full time and just hope, not hope but work to stay straight because when it comes right down to it that is my first goal, I guess. Just keep myself clean because I know if I start getting high again, everything else will just go in time and in my case a short period of time. So staying straight for me is about my biggest goal. If I do that anything else I want will come, as I say, in due time also.

Case Study 2

R. C. A.

White – Male – 17
Single
10th Grade Education
Character disorder (inadequate personality with psycho-sexual confusion)
Inability to adjust socially and vocationally characterized by drug abuse

Referral Source

Bob was referred to the Department of Vocational Rehabilitation by Dr. Jim Hancock of the Adolescent Clinic at City Hospital. In the initial interview, Bob was seen as a desperate, confused young man. He had recently dropped out of school because of his inability in adjusting to the school environment. Bob had been followed by Dr. Hancock since he was seven.

Social Data

Bob is a seventeen year old male. He comes from a middle class socio-economic background. His family consists of six members; his father, age fifty-two, his mother, age forty-five, his sister nineteen, and his two brothers, John, fifteen and Frank, age twelve. His father is athletic and is apparently a fairly successful man in the measures utilized in our culture. He is an engineer with a local firm and is financially stable. His mother is a housewife. She apparently is the only family member to show concern for Bob. In a counseling session with the rehabilitation counselor, Bob freely poured forth a tirade of verbal abuse toward his sister and his father but avoided speaking of his mother in any fashion. He described his youngest brother as the best adjusted member of the family and the one sibling toward whom he has the greatest affection.

Bob stated that he became interested in drugs when he was in high school. He began using marijuana in the ninth grade; "it calmed me down." He moved from grass to harder drugs such as LSD and Smack. This discussion concerning drugs and tripping was spontaneous and unsolicited by the counselor. He seems to be obsessed with the utilization of withdrawal through drugs. His last two trips, however, were not as good as the initial ones and he explained that he feels that there is a resistance to a breakthrough into something even more beautiful than he has experienced prior to this time. According to Bob, he had no trouble obtaining drugs in school. It was felt by the rehabilitation counselor that Bob enjoyed using drugs. Dr. Hancock informed the counselor that he has been working with Bob and his drug habit, but he has had little effect on Bob. He is still using LSD but has discontinued using Smack.

Bob presents a mod-type appearance. He is dressed in the *hippie* style of old blue jeans, flowered shirt, and with long hair. He however is dressed neatly and is clean. As far as hobbies, interests, etc. are concerned, Bob is apparently limited. He finds that listening to music is his only interest. He stated that he spends hours listening to the radio or stereo.

Medical Information

Bob's previous medical history reveals a well developed and nourished young man. He has never been seriously ill or treated in a hospital.

General Medical Examination

HEIGHT	6′1″
WEIGHT	145
EYES AND VISION	without glasses 20/200 with glasses 20/25
EARS AND HEARING	normal
NOSE, THROAT AND NECK	normal
MOUTH AND TEETH	normal
LYMPHATIC SYSTEM	normal
CHEST AND LUNGS	normal
HEART AND CIRCULATORY SYSTEM	normal
BLOOD PRESSURE	100/75

ABDOMEN–HERNIA	normal
GENITO-URINARY SYSTEM	normal
ANO–RECTAL	normal
NERVOUS SYSTEM	normal
ENDOCRINE SYSTEM	normal
SKIN	normal
VARICOSE VEINS	normal
SKELETAL OR ORTHOPEDIC	normal
LABORATORY	Blood Serology for Syphillis–Test used–VDRL/results non-reactive Urinalysis: Sp. Grav. 1.009;/albumen-neg./ sugar-neg./
Present limitation as to work capacity	none
Types of activity to be avoided	none

Educational Data

Bob dropped out of school when he was in the tenth grade. During his school history, Bob has been truant a great deal. He began to have difficulty in achievement and behaving in class when he was in the second grade. Psychological assessment and therapy were initiated. Bob was seen by his teachers as bright but due to his emotional problems he was having difficulty in achieving. His grades reflect his difficulty as he never achieved above a "C." The majority of grades were D's and F'S. His best subject was mathematics and his worst subject was English. He participated in no extracurricular activities and was an apparent "loner." Teacher observation reveals a boy unable to engage in successful peer relationships, with few friends, and a low self concept.

Vocationa Data

Bob reported difficulties of various sorts throughout his work history. He is currently working in a printing shop as a trainee. He stated that he hated his boss and the woman who works there but feels that the job is "tolerable." He has been unable to keep a job primarily because of differences with the supervisor or person in charge.

Psychological Data

Bob has had previous psychological evaluation once when he was seven years, eleven months of age and again when he was fifteen years old. He was referred at the age of seven because of his behavior in school. The tests administered were:

Wechsler Intelligence Scale for Children
Wide Range Achievement Test (reading)
Bender-Visual Motor *Gestalt* Test
Draw-A-Person
Rorschach

Observations of Behavior

Bob is an unusually polite boy in his mother's presence. After he is established in the testing room he no longer worries about his manners. His mother seemed a little reluctant to have him leave and was concerned about his being a "good" boy. Bob's first comment after he left his mother was, "Let's get this straight—I wish to be called Robert while I'm here." Later on he said I could call him whatever I wished. He said his feet were hot and removed his shoes but didn't take off his sweater. Initially he wriggled and squirmed, but this ceased as the session went on. He was also quite guarded.

Test Results:

Wechsler Intelligence Scale for Children:	
Verbal I.Q.	105
Performance I.Q.	111
Full Scale I.Q.	109
Wide Range Achievement Test:	
Reading Grade:	3.6

Bob's intellectual functioning is average at present though his development is rather uneven. He is blocked in his learning ability. His disturbing feelings are preventing him from attending to everyday learning experiences and are causing him to judge social situations emotionally rather than rationally. His difficulty with attention causes him to be inconsistent in his successes on various problems. In spite of this he manages to function in the above average range in many areas of his development. His potential is probably above average or better.

Bob is a boy who feels different from the other children. He sees himself as lowly, bad and incomplete. Thus, his thinking is non-conforming. He is a child who is completely overwhelmed by striving parents who demand that he achieve socially and intellectually and that he carefully control his impulses. He feels forced and pressured beyond his capabilities and experiences anxiety and insecurity when he behaves as a child. He is very frightened that he will be hurt and rejected as a result of his parents' domination and demands. He feels that he is being rejected by an overprotective, punitive mother and he wants very badly to receive love and attention.

Bob is experiencing intense feelings of hostility and destructive impulses which he tries hard to control – at times in a pedantic way. He is compulsively trying to structure his environment and fight it indirectly; however, he is often forced to withdraw and live out his impulses in fantasy.

He tends to stress social situations and to rigidly control himself in them, but he feels so inadequate, insecure, and fearful of being hurt that he stands off. He is afraid of others and afraid his hostility will spill out into overt behavior. Bob seems to "act out" his feelings in more indirect ways such as through enuresis, "hanging around" his mother, and being a school problem. These situations bring him the attention he so badly wants.

There seems to be a vicious circle going on here. His parents won't let him be himself and have young boy fun. He in turn frustrates their perfectionistic strivings.

At the age of fifteen, Bob was referred for psychological evaluation by his parents and school officials because of his absenteeism from school and his inability to socialize.

Tests Administered

Wechsler Intelligence Scale for Children

Wide Range Achievement Test
Bender-*Gestalt* Visual Motor Drawing Test
Rorschach Test

Test Interpretations

On the WISC he obtained a Verbal I.Q. of 106, a Performance I.Q. of 106 resulting in a Full Scale I.Q. of 107. All of these scores fall in the upper end of the average range of intelligence with some of the subtests reaching into the bright normal range. These results are very similar to those obtained on previous testing, suggesting that no basic deterioration or impairment in intellectual functioning has occurred but that he has been able to maintain himself on a fairly uniform level; however, as seen in 1960, present results also display the uneven development of intellectual functioning with low scores in areas suggesting some blocking in learning efficiency.

Achievement testing with the Wide Range Achievement Test showed him to be reading at the beginning of the 12th grade level, with spelling at the beginning of the 10th grade level, and arithmetic being in the mid-sixth grade level. His reading in terms of his present grade placement is about three years ahead of this grade with spelling being about one year ahead. There is marked underachievement in the area of mathematics. Here he showed a very erratic, careless approach, a fearfulness of the subject matter so that he blocked even from displaying having learned the basic arithmetic calculations and instead guessed and was very inaccurate.

Visual motor functioning as assessed on the Bender showed him to again be quite critical about himself although he tended to adhere quite well to the reality of the figures suggesting on the whole he can regulate himself fairly well though elapses occur particularly around situations related to authority-like figures. It was noted that in the memory component few of the figures containing female components were recalled and on one figure where he did remember there was a good deal of pressure and anxiety in the area of the figure where there was contact between the male-female components. The figures were rather reduced in size reflecting the very inadequate feelings he has about himself and how he interprets many things about himself as meaning this too.

It was on the more projective instruments that the basic distrust and suspiciousness of people emerged. Here he displayed much social anxiety and hypersensitivity in his relationships to others. He is quite apprehensive and hostile toward others, feeling that he is being looked upon, judged, demeaned in their eyes and has lived for a long time with very marked convictions of inadequacy about himself. One result has been a tendency to avoid social interactions, to run from situations which might highlight failures or which pose threats to him of such a nature. Yet, there is a good deal of guilt and there is the underlying image of himself as being bad which he then projects and sees himself as being rejected and hurt by others. There is a strong feeling of being spied upon or of being constantly under the scrutiny of others and that he is always coming off second best. His sensitivity is to such a point that he is ready to interpret stressful situations as always hurtful to him, and he may displace the anger resulting from these feelings of helplessness onto those less able than he, such as his siblings.

The most recent psychological evaluation was at the request of the rehabilitation counselor. Evaluation procedures used were:

Wechsler Adult Intelligence Scale
Bender-Visual Motor *Gestalt* Test
Wide Range Achievement Test
Rorschach

Test Results:

WAIS:

Information	11	Digit Symbol	9
Digit Span	10	Object Assembly	16
Comprehension	13	Picture Completion	11
Vocabulary	12	Picture Arrangement	13
Arithmetic	11	Block Design	17
Similarities	13		

Verbal IQ–115 Performance IQ–123 Full Scale IQ–119

Bob is seen as an extremely lonely young man. The most positive figure currently is the rehabilitation counselor. He spoke highly of him but also reported that he had nothing to offer the counselor. He seems symbiotic in his interpersonal relationships and tends to cling to any figure to whom he relates positively but also without conscious awareness tends to manipulate the situations simultaneously to fill his needs.

Bob mentioned his drug involvement as a matter of fact. He stated that he enjoyed the "highs" from Speed and LSD. He obviously enjoys talking about himself and finds it very difficult to become engrossed in a task or discussion of a theory or an individual with the exception of the relation to his life space and his experience directly.

On the WAIS Bob attained a verbal intelligence quotient of 115, (bright normal range), a performance quotient of 123 (superior range), and a full scale quotient of 119 (upper limit of bright normal range). There were no indications of organic impairment of the central nervous system at the present time, but the data were characterized by significant inter and intra-test variance which is suggestive of the interference of emotional maladaptive behavioral patterns. The scores were slightly higher than those achieved in previous psychological evaluations.

Bob experienced no difficulty in the identification of essential details, and as mentioned previously, he performed at the highest level possible in the reproduction of abstract designs. He also performed at a superior level in the construction of a meaningful *Gestalt* from component parts. His lower score was manifested in a slightly below average capacity to acquire and reproduce written symbols at a rapid rate. There were no deficiencies in abilities to integrate and synthesize material; to the contrary, psycho-motor skills are excellent and indicate superior capacities in this area.

The data from the Bender-*Gestalt* were not indicative of any difficulty in psycho-motor functioning or central nervous system impairment from organic etiology, but reflect the emotional disturbance which pervades the personality structure.

On the Wide Range Achievement Test, Bob performed in reading and spelling at current grade level or above, but he was not as proficient in arithmetic skills. In reading he attained a grade level of 15.3, in spelling a grade level of 10.7 and in arithmetic a grade level of 8.0. This data, in the area of reading especially, is commensurate with the intellectual potential indicated by the WAIS, and obviously if the emotional problems could be alleviated sufficiently, he could complete the necessary work for a college degree.

The projective data revealed a youngster characterized by a vivid and brilliant fantasy life in which he tends to satisfy passively many needs which he cannot fulfill actively. He is highly introverted and finds little satisfaction with people; in fact he has been disappointed over so many years that he has become highly negativistic in his reactions to ward off close interpersonal relationships which he feels will undoubtedly bring pain. Bob has the capacity for adequate reality ties and for the perception of the world in an ordinary manner, but under levels of stress tolerated fairly well by most people he tends to withdraw into a make believe environment of his own making rather than risk the involvement of emotional relationships. When this occurs he tends to be somewhat dramatic and bizarre in his appraisal of external situations and perceives significant others as threatening and weird, destructive giants. He perceives his father as a falsely destructive figure who "puts on a face." Toward his mother he symbolically and unconsciously associates the ideals of two opposing forces pulling against each other with ultimate goals of his annihilation. This is overwhelming for him. He tends to feel that if his own emotions are turned loose, they will result in a disaster area. Although Bob talked superficially about the need of a "chick," he also explained that he needed one "with a lot of problems." He actually is looking for a relationship in which he will not be threatened. He perceives others as so much more adequate than he that it is very difficult for him to find anyone who will permit comfortable associations without the possibility of rejection.

At the present time it is out of the question to consider mature heterosexual relationships, since he is psychosexually immature and extremely disturbed in patterns of interpersonal interaction. He has not developed constructive and acceptable means of expressing hostility and tends to project the causes for his problems onto those in the world about him. He has the capacity to empathize and to relate positively to others, but the emotional disturbances hampered development in this area. There are natural residual problems which center around parental figures, but he seems much more threatened by those centering upon the maternal relationships than those with the father figure. It seems that the central disturbance occurred earlier in this youngster's life, probably during his infancy, and there are indications that depth therapy would probably accomplish more for Bob than anything else, but it is necessarily an expensive, time consuming process.

Eligibility

Psychological and psychiatric evaluation reveals disability of behavior disorder characterized by interference from severely maladaptive emotional and behavioral patterns. These characteristics have resulted in academic failure, school dropout, inability to engage in successful peer relationships, very few interpersonal relationships, and an unrealistically low self concept. He has not developed constructive and acceptable means of expressing hostility.

The above conditions of maladjustment and failure are of sufficient severity to constitute a substantial handicap to employment.

Extended evaluation will allow for a more comprehensive and perceptive insight regarding this client's dynamics from both the counselor's and client's point of view. It will also allow for psychiatric assistance. These observations are positively indicated if a realistic and helpful determination is to be made by the counselor as to his rehabilitation potential.

Case Study 3

A. B. T.

Negro – Male – 18
Single
10th Grade Education
Drug abuse characterized by an inability to adjust vocationally and socially

Referral Source

Andrew was referred to the Department of Vocational Rehabilitation by the Social Service Bureau with a drug abuse problem. He had a $104.00 a day habit. Andrew was an eighteen year old black male with a 10th grade education at the time of referral.

Social Evaluation

Andrew's drug problem began in 1969, about the time of his mother's divorce action against his stepfather. As noted, Andrew's parents are divorced. The stepfather lives in a neighboring town. The stepfather is 35 to 40 percent disabled and without work. Andrew's mother was forced to work as a maid in a high school. She went for an examination for what was expected to be pregnancy but was found to be a tumor. An operation followed with an ensuing loss of income to the family. During his mother's illness, Andrew was shot five times in what appeared to be a gang war. His being a "pusher" probably had something to do with the shooting. Andrew is the oldest child in the family.

Psychological Evaluation

Andrew was given the A–B–L–E (Adult Basic Learning Examination). He received the following scores:

Vocabulary	9.0+
Spelling	8.7
Arithmetic Computation	9.0
Arithmetic Problem Solving	7.0
Arithmetic Total	7.2

These scores indicate that Andrew has a high level of retention evidently not hindered by his years out of school. His motivation is high and he wants to continue his education. Andrew wants a second chance at life since up to this point his life has only been emotionally troubled. His past problems seem to have been mainly instigated by environmental factors. Andrew is interested in a GED preparatory program. Following a high school GED equivalent, Andrew desires to attend a local business college and study business management.

The results of the A–B–L–E indicate that Andrew will probably be able to complete the high school equivalency diploma. His regular high school class will graduate in June, 1972. He should complete his GED by then. Encouragement coupled with Andrew's high motivation should enable him to do well in the business school. Some individual instruction seems to be indicated, but overall, the indications for success are positive.

Andrew was also given the Revised Beta Examination to determine I.Q. He received a score of 101.

Medical Evaluation

On January 26, 1972, Andrew was given a medical examination. It was found that he needed only glasses. Otherwise his health was good. He had only the normal childhood diseases. He is currently on a local methadone program for relief of his drug abuse problem. Before the methadone program he had snorted heroin for approximately 8–10 months and had started shooting heroin on a regular basis. His mother and father were aware of the drug problem. Aside from the gunshot wounds indicated earlier, from which he has recovered, these were the significant findings in the medical examination.

Vocational Evaluation

Andrew has no real vocational history. He expresses interest in business vocations.

Educational Evaluation

Andrew made average grades until he started on drugs. As tests indicate he has retained much factual knowledge from his high school years. He indicates a desire to finish high school and to go to business school.

Narrative

Andrew was referred by the Social Service Bureau. His mother is on welfare, which explains the Social Service Bureau's knowledge of Andrew. Andrew is the oldest of four children. He has three brothers, 13, 15, 16.

Andrew is currently on methadone treatments. He is also working on his GED high school equivalent. His motivation is high and indications are that he will successfully complete his GED. Andrew then wants to go to a local business college and study business management.

The Department of Vocational Rehabilitation will continue to aid Andrew as he proceeds toward his vocational goal. His application to business school has been accepted.

Case Study 4

M. J. J.

White – Female – 18
Single
High School Graduate
Passive-Aggressive Personality Trait Disturbance (Aggressive mixed type with depression)
Drug abuse characterized by an inability to adjust vocationally and socially

Referral Source

Jane was referred to the Department of Vocational Rehabilitation after her release from the State Mental Hospital. The vocational rehabilitation counselor had extreme difficulty in locating this individual. Several attempts were made to contact Jane by telephone and home visits. She was previously employed as a switch board operator in Fort Worth, Texas. She began to experience extreme states of anxiety and nervousness which resulted in her leaving this job and returning to this state. Once home with her parents, she was hospitalized.

Social Data

Jane is an eighteen year old, attractive woman. She is living with her parents, and her two brothers, age sixteen and twelve. Her father is employed with the postal service and both he and her mother are college graduates. Her two brothers are attending high school. She comes from very middle class socio-economic background. As stated by her mother, Jane, as a child had a friendly disposition but later became disappointed in certain people. This disappointment led to difficulty in controlling her temper. Her personality as a child was good. She was at ease around people but became afraid, shy and mistrusting of others. In her early teens she would go out of her way to make friends, but when she was rejected she would withdraw.

It was in this period of her life that she began complaining about stomach aches and difficulty in breathing. When she was taken to a local hospital for a checkup the doctors were unable to find any abnormalities or diagnose the trouble.

She was of the Baptist faith and attended church regularly as a child. As she began to participate in church activities, she began to feel that some of the teenagers did not like her. She also became disappointed in two of her pastors and withdrew from church related activities. She presently rejects any religion.

Jane presented a depressed appearance. On each occasion that the vocational rehabilitation counselor met her she was somewhat unattractively dressed. It was quite obvious that she was trying to dress according to the latest fashion, and at the same time managed to look very unattractive.

Jane admits to the use of drugs, including heroin and barbituates but maintains that she is not using them now. She was arrested for possession of marijuana but reports that the charges were dismissed. She has been peripherally involved in a number of anti-establishment incidents, but according to Jane, has never been formally charged with anything. She believes that the police are harassing her and also believes some of her friends are police informers.

Jane reports considerable difficulties and friction between her and her parents. Most of her problems revolve around her sexual activity and bizarre behavior in the home. Jane states that she likes "sex" and on occasion has had intercourse with several men in the same evening. She has brought her boyfriends into her parents' home for the evening and this has been very upsetting to them. Once during a family argument, Jane locked herself in her bathroom for an entire month, sneaking out only at night in order to obtain food.

She is interested in political movement concerned with an individual's rights. She likes English as a school subject and does read when she finds time.

Educational Data

Jane completed the twelfth grade of high school. She felt that she had been an outcast in school. However, she maintained honor roll status while in school, excelling in math and English. She attended City University for one semester but failed to pass any courses.

Medical Data

Jane complains of depression and insomnia. Other than these complaints, she is in good general health. Her illnesses consisted of normal childhood diseases such as measles, chicken pox, mumps, sore throats and so on. However, later in life she complained about stomach aches and difficulties in breathing. Doctors were unable to find any abnormalities or diagnose the problem.

Although she has a history of drug involvement, she apparently did not become physically addicted. She also states that she had never used a "dirty" needle when shooting heroin.

General Medical Examination

HEIGHT	66 3/4 "
WEIGHT	141 1/2 lbs.
EYES AND VISION	normal
EARS AND HEARING	normal
NOSE, THROAT, NECK	normal
MOUTH AND TEETH	normal
LYMPHATIC SYSTEM	normal
CHEST AND LUNGS	normal
HEART AND CIRCULATORY SYSTEM	normal
BLOOD PRESSURE	120/60
ABDOMEN-HERNIA	normal
GENITO-URINARY SYSTEM	normal
ANO-RECTAL	normal
NERVOUS SYSTEM	normal
ENDOCRINE SYSTEM	normal
SKIN	normal
VERICOSE VEINS	negative
SKELETAL OR ORTHOPEDIC	normal
BLOOD SEROLOGY FOR SYPHILIS	negative

URINALYSIS;	Sp. Grav. N S Q Albumen 2+ Sugar 0
PRESENT LIMITATION AS TO WORK CAPACITY	no restriction
TYPES OF ACTIVITY TO BE AVOIDED	none
WORKING CONDITIONS TO BE AVOIDED	none

Examination by psychiatrist is advisable for completeness of diagnosis

Psychological History

The female admissions staff conference at the State Mental Hospital found Jane's condition to be characterized by some resentful, antagonistic feelings toward her father and brothers, ideas of reference, and paranoid flavors. In the interview, Jane stated, "everyone makes fun of me and I can't keep any friends. I don't know what I want to be. I couldn't get a job, I don't do anything, don't go anywhere, just sit home and cry." "I ain't feeling good and that's for sure, I couldn't sleep last night." She freely admitted that she has two younger brothers and she blames her father for letting them walk all over her, letting them talk back to her. She has a pessimistic and low opinion of herself. Jane would like to get married but she doesn't have any boy friends and she would like to have kids, but she can't get any of these things. She appears to be easily agitated, tempermental, and depressed. There is no evidence of hallucinations or delusions. She seemed to be in good contact and is fully aware of her surroundings. Her memory is preserved in all three spheres.

Diagnosis

Adjustment Reaction to Adolescence.

Recommendation

Treat with anti-depressent – Etrafon, plus tranquilizer Mellaril or Thorazine.

Jane was released from the State Mental Hospital after two months of intensive treatment. It was at this time that she was referred to the Department of Vocational Rehabilitation.

A battery of tests was given consisting of the:

Bender-Visual Motor *Gestalt* Test
Wechsler Adult Intelligence Scale
Wide Range Achievement Test
Rorschach Ink Blot Test

Results:

WAIS	VIQ	112	–(Verbal)
	PIQ	111	–(Performance)
	F.S.I.Q.	112	–(Full Scale)

The Bender *Gestalt* Data evidenced no organically based impairment or dysfunction of the central nervous system.

The data of the Wide Range Achievement correlated relatively well with Jane's intellectual capacity and educational level with the exception of arithmetic performance. She attained a reading level of 14.7, a spelling level of 11.6, and an arithmetic level of 8.0. Without question Jane has developed high level academic skills which will be advantageous either in the acquisition of higher education or in vocational planning.

The projective data is indicative of a lonely, isolated, young woman with tremendous unfulfilled emotional needs. To attempt satisfaction of these, she relies heavily on a rich fantasy life. She perceives the environment as most people do, and one of the primary problems centers upon sexual confusion which has probably resulted from the patterns of parental behavior. She tends to see the female figure as somewhat stronger than that of the male and cannot integrate ideas of masculinity and feminity with proper behavioral patterns.

Abstract

Abstract from the psychological interviews and observations:

In the beginning of the interview Jane had a somewhat wooden expression on her face which led me to believe that we might be dealing with possible schizophrenic disorder. However, fortunately she became more secure in the interview and relaxed.

Psychiatric Evaluation

This young girl presents a paradoxical picture. In a way she feels extremely lonely and different from other people. She never had a close relationship with her mother and has more or less stayed aloof from her father. The paradox in this girl is that inside she feels a failure, different, unattractive and undesirable but at the same time she feels superior. After some prodding, she revealed that she had used a potpourri of drugs in a form of youth rebellion.

Diagnosis

Passive aggressive – dependent – aggressive mixed type personality.

Recommendations

Jane still has quite a confusion about her own identity goals and appears lonely. For this reason I feel this young girl would certainly benefit from psychotherapy and when this was explored, it appeared that she was highly motivated for this. The psychotherapy is recommended in two blocks of twelve treatments each.

Abstracts

Abstracts of the Psychotherapy Session

After the first twelve sessions Jane was still having a difficult time in controlling impulses especially in the sexual field. She cooperates well and has been able to talk about her feelings which have bothered her for an extended period of time. The diagnosis remains the same as to the basic personality.

Vocational Data

Jane has had only two jobs in her employment history. The first was as a switchboard operator in Texas. She was fired from this job because of her emotional status.

When the patient returned from the State Hospital, she got a job at Lendy's Restaurant as a cashier and short-order cook. She was promised to be made manager, but someone else got the job and she quit because of the disappointment and too much work. Since that time she has not been working, staying at home, sleeping all day in the beginning but now is getting anxious and restless.

Eligibility

Client has an emotional disability diagnosed as passive aggressive–dependent-aggressive mixed type personality, which is hampering her social and emotional adjustment as well as her intellectual and performance capacities. Dr. V. in his psychiatric evaluation of the client indicated that she was in need of and could benefit from psychotherapy and unless she became involved in this, a vocational objective that would be commensurate with capabilities and interests would not be workable.

With appropriate psychotherapy this client who is characterized by superior intellectual capacity would be able to maintain the emotional tolerance level to achieve successfully in college setting which is her desire in order to reach her vocational potential. A general medical indicates that other than the depression, client is in good physical condition.

The limitations resulting from the above described disability constitute a vocational handicap to employment as well as to means needed to be employed in order for client to obtain vocational skills commensurate with her capabilities. She has confusion about her own identity goals as often vacillates between vocational objectives. She is unable to tolerate stress and constructive criticism. Client has lost employment due to emotional instability as well as the fact that the job which was waitress work was beneath her intellectual functioning. While she is college material as far as her intellectual capacity is concerned, at this point she definitely does not have the emotional stability to handle the pressure of college.

Case Study 5

J. A. S.

White – Female – 18
Single
High School Graduate
Drug abuse characterized by an inability to adjust vocationally and socially

Referral Source

Miss S. was referred to the Department of Vocational Rehabilitation by Dr. B. of the Adolescent Clinic City Hospital. She is presently being followed at the Adolescent Clinic for adjustment reaction to adolescence, characterized by drug abuse. She has been in the methadone program and has received guidance and counseling.

Social Data

Miss S. is an eighteen year old white female. Her family background is less than ideal. Her parents have recently divorced, and since then she has been on her own a great deal. Her father is an alcoholic now living out of this state. She is the youngest of three children all of whom have experienced problems in living. She feels that her mother is not very concerned about her actions and cares very little about her. She and her mother argue almost constantly.

Miss S. was arrested for drug abuse. She was caught using heroin. She is presently out on bond and has been referred for a physical examination and evaluation of her drug dependence before she went to court. She was placed on probation with the stipulation that she enter a drug treatment program. Before the arrest, she had used heroin regularly for the past six months. She has used a variety of drugs including cocaine, marijuana, LSD, heroin. She had been exposed to hepatitis two weeks before her arrest. One of the boys she and her friend were sharing their "works" unit with had hepatitis. In spite of all her troubles, she did manage to graduate from high school by going in the summer.

Medical Data

Miss S. was seen by a clinic physician for a general examination and for determination of a physical addiction. She states that she feels fine with no physical complaints. She has been exposed to hepatitis through the use of a friend's dirty needle. 10 cc of gamma globulin were given as a prophylaxis. Her general appearance is that of a thin, healthy, adolescent female.

GENERAL PHYSICAL EXAMINATION:

HEIGHT	64″
WEIGHT	117½ lbs.
VISION	normal
SKIN – Color	normal
Eruptions	mild
Pallor	no
Icterus	no
HAIR	oily
EYES	normal
NOSE – Obstruction	no
Sinus Tenderness	no
MOUTH AND THROAT	
Oral Hygiene	poor
Gums	caries present
Tonsils	normal
LYMPH GLANDS	normal
THORAX	normal
LUNGS	clear to auscultation
HEARING	o.k.
EPISTAXIS	no
HAY FEVER	no
TOOTHACHE	no
CHEST PAIN	no
COUGH	mild
APPETITE	fair
ABDOMINAL PAIN	no
DYSURIA	no

B.P.	120/70
HEART RSR	normal
ABDOMEN	soft
GENITALIA	stage of development-stage V
NEUROLOGICAL	gait–good
	strength–good
	balance–good
	pilonidal sinus–normal
	coordination–good
	reflexes–normal
FEET	normal
PERSONALITY TRAITS	tense
	restless

Positive findings revealed needle scars on both arms. It was the opinion of this physician that she is physically addicted, needs psychiatric referral and at some time gamma globulin as a prophylaxis for possible hepatitis. The physical impression is that of a young, healthy female with the exception of needle marks. It is also recommended that she be placed in the Methadone program.

Educational Data

Miss S. has not done well in school, especially in high school. Her grades were below average – D's and F's; however, she did manage to graduate from high school by attending summer school to make up for credits lost during the regular year. A transcript of her high school performance indicated that Miss S. was not involved in any extra-curricular activities.

Psychological Data

Upon completion of the medical, Miss S. was referred to the Guidance Clinic for psychiatric therapy. A battery of tests consisting of the Wechsler Adult Intelligence Scale, Bender-Visual-Motor *Gestalt* Test, Wide Range Achievement Test-Reading Section, House-Tree-Person Drawing, and the Rorschach Test was given.

Miss S. is a thin, brown haired, brown eyed girl who was pleasant and responsive and who had a tendency to talk in a dunning fashion and to play with her rather greasy, straight hair. She presented a rather dull, uninteresting physical appearance in that she was dressed somewhat sloppily in brown, short culottes, a short brown suede jacket and loafers. However, upon closer inspection, she was actually a rather pretty girl with pretty eyes and a pleasant smile which seemed all to infrequent. Miss S. sat sprawled in her chair and seemed unaware of her bare thighs being exposed, yet she was overly anxious to keep her chest covered up with her jacket; she almost seemed to make a "thing" out of keeping her jacket closed. She appeared to enjoy the testing, and as time went on became more comfortable and was able to laugh; at such times her eyes sparkled and she was a very attractive girl. She talked at length about wanting to leave her mother and go out on her own but at the same time feeling guilty since she was the last child. She thinks her father is a "nice guy" but does not like living with him. She snickered and became evasive while talking about her father; and gave the impression that there is far more involved here than meets the eye. She spoke of her feelings of depression, her having been caught and her sexual experiences with various boys in a curiously detached, depersonalized way. She rationalized having been caught as "the vice squad is corrupt," and that "this city is too big and unfeeling." She considers the people where her father lives as being "warm," friendly, loving and judging people for their "inner self." She further says that people who take drugs because of nothing better to do are much like her.

Miss S. is able to function on the bright normal level of general intelligence according to her full scale I.Q. of 117; her verbal score of 114 and her performance scale of 122. She has difficulty in those areas which require concentration and synthetic ability on visual-motor tasks; her concentration has a tendency to come and go with the results that the quality of her performance fluctuates. On the other hand, she was able to demonstrate superior social comprehension and judgment in a hypothetical situation. Her *gifted* score on the subtest which involved attention to environmental essentials suggest that she is overly concerned with things rather than people. Other areas tested generally fell in the bright normal range. Certainly this is a very bright girl whose intellectual functioning tends to be somewhat erratic because her intellectual energies are being dissipated by emotional concerns. Miss S. is presently reading on the 10.2 grade level, which gives her a standard score of 103 and places her in the 58th percentile for one of her age group. This is considerably below her level of intellectual functioning and is an example of her problem with utilizing her intellectual ability in every day living situations. At this time there does not seem to be any indication of a central nervous system dysfunction. Her test results are those of a bright, sensitive, withdrawn, immature, and somewhat regressed individual who is maintaining a passive-feminine orientation in her approach to her world as a defense against inward strivings toward destructive fighting and sadistic impulses which actually terrify her. She is one who feels depressed, constrained, and trapped and has a sense of not being alive and of watching life pass her by at this time. Actually, she feels unable to participate in life and goes to great lengths to project the blame on others, circumstances, places, etc. so that she will not be forced to recognize her depressed, inadequate state. She entertains many feelings of inner emptiness and futility.

This is a girl who has much sex-role confusion and who appears to be experiencing panic over a sexual identity crisis. She is confused about who and what she is, is frightened and guilty at her narcissistic and autoerotic urges. She often provokes situations such as seducing the male in order to later resent and blame him for the predicament in which she finds herself. When she deals with the male, it is in terms of her feelings of intense hostility, and her tendency to deal with males as well as people in general in a sneaky, self-centered and manipulatory way. She does have some feelings of panic concerning the male inasmuch as she has a tendency to project on to him her intense sadistic, destructive, aggressive and annihiliating impulses.

Miss S. views the female with a sense of anxiety; she feels erratic about the female and has a tendency to be evasive and avoidant when she deals with the female. She attempts to defend against her sensual impulses toward the female by projecting them on to others. Actually, she remains at the narcissistic level and attempts to cope with her homosexual urges by fleeing to heterosexual involvement in the way of defense. She is one who has intense dependency and oral needs, who is weak and passive, yet who has feelings which are too hot to handle and impulses which threaten to be out of control. This is a girl who wants and needs controls and who is presently experiencing panic over an imminent loss of control. She identifies with people on an immature, self-centered level, but has little real sensitivity to and concern about people.

It is recommended that she be placed in a living situation which imposes strict controls such as a school away from home, or if this is not feasible, that she be hospitalized. In any event she should be involved in psychotherapy preferably of a group therapy nature which will be intensive. It is felt that this girl is experiencing an identity crisis and is fence-sitting at this time; thus, which way she moves will depend upon the treatment and living situation which she experiences within the next year or two.

Vocational Data

Miss S. has never been employed, full time or during the summers. She has expressed an interest in pursuing a career as a social worker and would like to go to college.

Eligibility

Miss S. received a medical evaluation in December, 1971 and was found to be within normal physical limits with no physical restrictions or activities to be avoided. Client was noted to be on the Methadone program due to drug abuse. Based on a psychiatric and psychological evaluation this client is seen as currently demonstrating numerous characteristics of a behavioral disorder. Client has been involved in drug abuse, dropout behavior, and currently has experienced anxiety and depression due to her condition. This condition constitutes a substantial handicap to employment. With the provision of appropriate vocational rehabilitation services a favorable outcome is anticipated for this rehabilitation plan.

Vocational Objective

SOCIAL WORKER – Since that date of the initial interview this client has received counseling and guidance. Based on the diagnostic information obtained in this rehabilitation program, this client has been receiving attention from the Adolescent Clinic at City Hospital and the Guidance Clinic. These institutions have provided the diagnostic information which indicates at the current time that this individual is ready for the provision of appropriate rehabilitation services towards the above indicated vocational objective. In order to achieve this goal, she must receive formal vocational academic training within a local facility: tuition, necessary fees, and books. From the rehabilitation counselor in this case, she will receive maintenance, clothes, and transportation in order to participate in the rehabilitation program. At the appropriate time in this individual's rehabilitation plan she will be placed within competitive employment and follow-up provided in order to insure an adequate vocational adjustment. The estimated duration of this plan at the current time is four years.

Over-All Plan and Financing

Tuition – one semester	$ 235.00
Activity Fee – one semester	12.00
Health Fee – one semester	20.00
Books – one semester	50.00
Psychotherapy – 15 sessions @ $30.00	450.00
Maintenance – 4 months @ $80.00	320.00
Clothes	75.00
Transportation	45.00
Methadone – 5 months @ $47.00	235.00
TOTAL	$1,442.00

Case Study 6

L. B. J.

Black – Male – 40
Married
9th Grade Education
Behavioral disorder with acting out tendencies. Also, drug abuse characterized by an inability to adjust vocationally and socially

Referral Source

Mr. J. was referred to vocational rehabilitation by the Welfare and Institutions State Penitentiary when he was released on parole. He has had a history of poor community adjustment which resulted in criminal acts. In addition, Mr. J. has been addicted to heroin and at one time was a client of the drug rehabilitation center at Lexington, Kentucky. He is currently on the city Methadone program. His vocational background is sporatic due to his legal involvements and also to his drug addiction.

Social Data

Mr. J. is a forty year old, black male. He is married with no children. In actuality, his wife is the bread winner in the family. She supports her husband by working as a nurse in a VA Hospital. Mr. J. is close to his parents who are now on welfare. His father was at one time a Baptist minister. He has eight brothers and two sisters all of whom are employed with the exception of two brothers that are heavy drinkers.

Mr. J. states that his hobbies are fishing and doing household chores. Mr. J. has also become very interested in the Islamic religion. For the last ten years he has read and studied about the religion and has recently changed from Baptist to the Islamic faith.

Mr. J. has spent the past twenty years in and out of prison. At the age of twenty, he was arrested and convicted of breaking and entering. He was sentenced to a year at the state farm. During this year, he escaped but was quickly apprehended. He was released after serving an extra six months for his escape. Four years later, while on a fishing trip he and two other friends maliciously "beat up" a game warden. Apparently he was giving them a ticket for fishing without a license. Mr. J. was convicted and sentenced to eleven years at the State Penitentiary. He served seven years and two months and then was released on parole. Within the year, he had jumped parole and left for New York. It was during the next two years in New York City that he began experimenting with drugs, especially heroin. After three and a half years, he was apprehended and returned to the State Penitentiary where attempts were made to get him into a local drug treatment program. He refused to go to this hospital but did eventually attend the Federal Health Service Hospital in Lexington, Kentucky. These rehabilitation efforts failed and he was returned to the State Penitentiary. Again he was paroled but violated it by his reinvolvement with drugs. While in his last year of serving time as a parole violator he was assigned as a trustee, an honor position, to the Welfare Building. The counselors felt that during this time, he had made a good record for himself.

Mr. J. was a meek and mild mannered individual who speaks softly and does not apparently possess a great deal of intelligence. He says he no longer has a drug problem since he has started taking Methadone and does not anticipate one in the future. He is interested in obtaining some type of training that will enable him to provide for himself and his wife.

Educational Data

Mr. J. completed the ninth grade. He said he had to drop out because of a family economic hardship. While in school he received grades of C's and D's. His interests while in high school were music and tailoring. He has not been in any adult training program, either on his own or while in prison.

Medical Data

A medical examination reported that Mr. J. has had a normal medical history and is presently in good medical condition. No abnormalities were recorded under section two which was filled out at the rehabilitation agency.

HEIGHT	5′8″
WEIGHT	167 lbs.
EYES	Rt/normal
	Lt./normal
Color Vision	normal
DISTANCE VISION	Rt/20/25
	Lt/20/25
EARS	Rt. 12
	Lt. 12
test used C128	tuning fork
MOUTH	normal
NOSE	normal
NECK	normal
LYMPHATIC SYSTEM	normal
LUNGS	clear
HEART	normal
BLOOD PRESSURE	110/84
PULSE	80
EDEMA	none

Psychological Data

Mr. J. has had a history of inability to adjust to society. In 1952 Dr. C. in a neuropsychiatric report concluded that J. was extremely emotionally unstable and impulsive and was given to erratic behavior. He is unable to profit by previous errors and allows free expression of his passive feelings. He is immature and hedonistic; possesses strong antisocial tendencies and is unable to gain any insight in this difficulty. In view of the present attitude, it is not probable that a clear future can be anticipated. In that same year the Revised Beta, Otis Quick Scoring Test and the Stenquist Mechanical Aptitude were administered.

Intelligence – within the normal range
Revised Beta – Mental Age 13-7 I.Q.–91 non-verbal
Otis Quick Scoring – Mental Age 11 I.Q.–73 verbal

Mr. J. would be capable of finishing high school. He lacks mechanical aptitude and is poor in the clerical areas. Mr. J. was felt to be of normal intelligence. Apparently he is able to adjust adequately under supervision but seems to have profited little from it. He continues to react impulsively, to choose poor associates and use very poor judgment. He reveals little insight, no remorse and has little apparent desire for self improvement. The prognosis continues to be poor and supervision is needed.

In a more recent psychological interview, Mr. J. presented a most unusual picture. He was conventionally groomed, his manner was equally appealing and had an unusual degree of sophistication, assertiveness, and resonance.

There is evidence of a dull normal intellectual endowment, but it is felt he makes full use of it when confronted with problems. Mr. J. is a characterologically damaged person, who is being rigidly controlled by a religious theme, who feels supressed and bound. At times he has shown an interest in auto mechanics, a field of study which he now wishes to explore. His level of aspiration and his level of functional ability seem quite compatable.

Vocational History

Mr. J.'s vocational history has been sporatic due to his incarcerations and drug addiction. In all jobs, he was a driver of some type. His first was as a fork lift operator with a tobacco factory in the city. He lost this job when he was convicted in breaking and entering. His next job was while he was an escapee in New York. His last job on the street was as a driver of a cement truck for a construction materials business in the city. He states that he would like to go back to driving some type of truck. Because of his various experience as a driver with several companies in the city, he feels he can drive "anything."

Eligibility

Mr. J. is an individual characterized by a behavioral disorder which has led to other attendent factors such as poor community relations, dropping out of school, criminal involvement and drug abuse.

Vocational Objective

AUTO MECHANIC – The justification for this objective was based on the client's normal physical limits with no restrictions or activities to be avoided. The client has stated a sincere and active interest in the above chosen field. Appropriate rehabilitation training is available within the area and he has been accepted for this training.

Based on a survey of the employment market within this area, there is a good demand for skills as indicated by this objective and employment will be no problem, after the successful completion of training.

Summary of Services

Since the date of the initial interview, Mr. J. has been provided with extensive diagnostic services. All information currently obtained indicates that this individual is ready for the provision of rehabilitation services. Based on an evaluation of this client by a local training facility, it has been found acceptable for this individual to successfully undertake the above indicated training. While in training, necessary tools and other types of expenses as deemed appropriate will be provided. After the successful completion of this individual's training, he will be placed in competitive employment and follow up will be provided in order to insure an adequate vocational adjustment. The overall duration of this plan at the current time is eight months.

OVER ALL COST AND PLANS FOR FINANCING:

Tuition-six months. @247.50/month	$1,485.00
Transportation	200.00
Textbooks	15.00
Work Clothes	75.00
Employment Tools	90.00

Vendor: City Technical Institute

Client has been referred to Social Service Bureau, Department of Welfare for subsistance allowance while undergoing training. Client was accepted for general relief by Welfare.

Case Study 7

B. B. T.

Negro – Male – 20
Single
High School Graduate
Drug abuse characterized by an inability to adjust vocationally and socially

Referral Source

Bernie was referred by the adolescent clinic of a local hospital as a behavioral problem characterized by drug abuse. He is twenty years old, single, and of the Negro race. He has been for several months on Methadone treatment for heroin addiction.

Social History

Bernie lives with his mother. In the past he has been shifted between mother and father, who are separated. He has four younger siblings, two brothers and two sisters. He earned only $150 per month working at a fast-food service establishment. He apparently shared this wealth with his family. His interests are basketball, music, girls, and "smack."

Psychological Data

Bernie was evaluated psychologically recently. The following evaluative procedures were used:

Bender-Visual Motor *Gestalt* Test
Wechsler Adult Intelligence Scale
Rorschach
Thematic Apperception Technique
Minnesota Multiphasic Personality Inventory

Bernie is presently functioning in the range of "average" to "bright normal" intelligence (Verbal I.Q. 112, Performance I.Q. 100, Full Scale WAIS I.Q. 108). Anxiety appears to interfere with his functioning, most noticeably on perceptual-motor tasks. There is no evidence of organic brain dysfunction discernible.

The personality evaluation indicates that Bernie is a very scared, anxious, sensitive, suspicious young man. Although he has the necessary intellectual skills to function effectively in a training program, the above indicated personality adjustment problems may interfere. Bernie feels too inadequate and inferior to assert himself or compete successfully. He expresses mostly negative attitudes which reflect active, impulsive, and destructive behavior to achieve his goals. He holds attitudes of contempt and derision toward women. He regards them as objects for his pleasure. He tells a story about "this guy who just finished raping this woman . . .." These attitudes result in Bernie being manipulative. He meets his goals by immature, impulsive, and hostile behavior. As a result Bernie's social behavior is inappropriate and nonconforming, his interpretation of situations are inaccurate to extremely poor.

The overall evaluation indicates that Bernie is experiencing severe adjustment difficulties. Although he has the intellectual capabilities for effective adjustment, his impulsive, hostile, irrational, non-conforming behavior interferes with general adjustment.

Medical History

Bernie had the normal childhood diseases. He had an appendectomy and a tonsillectomy. His only recorded accident was a slight concussion incurred while wrestling. Bernie's chief complaint at the medical examination was heroin addiction; "I need help." He had started on heroin four months previously, snorting and shooting.

The physical findings were all in normal ranges with the following exceptions: bilateral wheezes, heroin addiction. He was diagnosed as a heroin addict. It was recommended that he be referred to vocational rehabilitation and be started on Methadone treatments.

Vocational History

Bernie has worked intermittently on a variety of jobs since he graduated from high school in 1969. He, however, has no real skills. An interest in computers and machinery is indicated.

Educational History

Although of average and high average intelligence, Bernie's grades got progressively worse as he progressed through school. He started, as a freshman, with a C average; as a senior, he attained a D average. Bernie's absenteeism progressively increased from five days absence to thirty-five days. He repeated the twelfth grade.

Narrative

From the time Bernie went to the adolescent clinic at the hospital to his present participation in a computer school, he has shown positive direction and attitude. While he was associated with the hospital and now, Bernie has stayed off heroin with the aid of Methadone treatments. Bernie showed interest in computer school, so his rehabilitation counselor aided him in gaining admittance. He is still on Methadone treatments. Bernie is currently in computer school and being maintained by allowance from rehabilitation. He is highly motivated. His programming instructor says he is eager and shows an evident desire to learn. The instructor expects Bernie to successfully complete the course.

Case Study 8

H. P. D.

Black – Male – 33
Divorced
High School Graduate
Schizophrenic reaction, paranoid type with multiple drug abuse

Referral Source

Mr. D. was referred to the Department of Vocational Rehabilitation by the Department of Welfare and Institutions for help in finding some suitable employment. He had just been released from a local mental institution and listed as not mentally ill. The vocational rehabilitation counselor met with Mr. D. and arranged for a local physician to perform the physical examination. During the initial contact with Mr. D., there appeared to be no drug related problems; however, the physical examination found him to be using heroin. The rehabilitation counselor contacted Mr. D. and during the next interview he questioned him concerning his use of drugs. He denied any use of drugs at all. The counselor, at this time, contacted the local mental institution by letter for more information concerning the client.

Social Data

Mr. D. is a 33 year old black male with a Afro-haircut and a mustache. He presents a neat and clean dress and appearance. Mr. D. was born in 1939 in Richmond, Virginia. His father is fifty-two years of age, is in good health and works in a dry cleaning plant. His mother died in 1965 at the age of forty-four of hypertension and its complications. Upon graduating from high school, he entered the Signal Corps and was sent to Viet Nam. While there, he became a victim of a prolonged drug habit. The highest rank that he obtained was that of private. After he returned from Viet Nam he received a general discharge. Before he left for Viet Nam, Mr. D. married a girl who was seventeen at the time. One daughter was born to this union. Apparently the couple decided to marry after the child was born. They separated after two years of marriage with his wife gaining custody of the child. There is some legal doubt as to Mr. D's marriage or divorce. His wife is a nursing assistant and works at one of the local hospitals but not consistantly at any particular one. He says that he sees her occasionally.

Mr. D. experienced many different drugs but said he primarily used marijuana and heroin. Once in civilian life, he found it increasingly hard to procure drugs. As his habit increased he became increasingly uncontrollable. He became so violent and unmanageable while coming down off of heroin that he was committed to a mental institution by his family. He remained in this hospital for four months and then transferred to a different hospital that had drug treatment facilities. After he detoxed and functioned in a normal manner, he was released with no indication of a drug problem existing. The rehabilitation counselor again met with Mr. D. who admitted to a intermittent usage of drugs especially heroin along with hallucinogenics and barbiturates. With his consent he was placed on the methadone program. At present he is unemployed. He said that he has never worked to amount to anything since getting out of the service.

Medical Data

Mr. D. stated that he has no complaints except for what he calls "nerves." He is chronically nervous and has been so since he had a "nervous breakdown." This breakdown resulted in his hospitalization with the diagnosis being at that time, paranoid schizophrenic. He was discharged from the hospital following a four month hospitalization and was again diagnosed as paranoid schizophrenic. Three years later, Mr. D. had serum hepatitis secondary to infection with a non-sterile needle. He is still addicted to drugs. Other than the past indicated psychiatric history, the client has no history of confusion episodes, head trauma, or seizures. He has no problems with headaches, hallucinations, episodes of uncoordination or other neurological deficit.

Mr. D. has been on Mellaril and Valium. He stopped Mellaril about six months ago and ran out of Valium recently.

GENERAL APPEARANCE

This is a 32 year old black male who is well developed and well nourished with no acute distress.

PULSE	68
RESPIRATION	21
BLOOD PRESSURE	128/95
SKIN AND HAIR	Normal
HEAD	Normal in size and shape
EYES	Brown
TEETH	good
NECK	Thyroid not enlarged
SPINE	No deformity
CHEST	Lungs are clear to percussion and auscultation
HEART	Normal
Slight arteriosclerosis	
ABDOMEN	Negative
EXTREMITIES	No gross physical abnormalities
NEUROLOGICAL	No gross physical abnormalities
REFLEXES	present
WEIGHT	134 lbs.
HEIGHT	5′8″

IMPRESSIONS: Essentially negative physical examination

Psychiatric Data

Mr. D. is a person of average general ability. He is oriented as to person and time but not as to place. He says he has no desire to return to marijuana or to heroin. His memory for remote events is satisfactory, however, his memory for recent events is somewhat spotty due to his drug habit. He had hallucinations while he was taking heroin and some of the other drugs. He is guarded in mentioning all of the medications he has taken, but apparently he had run the whole gamut starting with marijuana and ending up with heroin. At the present time he has no hallucinations or delusions. He feels impotent, overwhelmed and almost helpless. He has been rejected for help by the VA and now he says that the state will not help him much longer with his drug problem. He thinks that he got into the drug habit because he was overworked. Mr. D. said that he had hepatitis and gonorrhea which he contracted in Viet Nam, and that when approached by a friend with medications to take, he felt like taking anything to get some relief from his pain and suffering. He appears to be of at least normal intelligence. His range of interest and store of general knowledge is within normal limits. His affect reveals slight depression. He says that he has had fleeting thoughts of suicide, but this was mainly when he was taking medications and he himself feels that he would never commit suicide. He is not considered to be a suicidal risk at this time. His comprehension and judgment are within normal limits. He has some understanding of his illness although he tends to "pass the buck." He has no insight into his problems.

Clinical Evaluation

Gross identification reveals a well developed and well nourished young male, who is slightly hostile and uncooperative. Mr. D's thinking is somewhat confused. He cannot subtract 7 from 100 serially. He knows the names of the last five presidents of the United States (Wechsler Intelligence Test). He is quite suspicious. His feelings seem to be one of slight depression. The clinical impression is that Mr. D. is a schizophrenic reaction, paranoid type.

Vocational Data

Since Mr. D's release from the army, he has done little work. He said he last worked as a common laborer. However, this did not last long because of his hospitalization. Mr. D. states his vocational interest is to be a welder.

Once placed in the methodone program, he entered a training program for welding. Mr. D. did not last long on either program. He went exactly one week to welding school and did not go in for his methadone but once during a two week span. The rehabilitation counselor made a trip to his house and found him in the process of leaving the home. He stated that he had gotten some "bad stuff" and was going to the hospital. The counselor offered to take him and he accepted. Mr. D. was admitted to the hospital and spent one week there under intensive care and was released the following week. Two days after his release from the hospital, he was fatally wounded in a gang war. It was suspected that he had gone to kill the person that had sold him the bad heroin, but he and his friends were surprised by another gang and the fight ensued, leaving Mr. D. fatally wounded and two others from either side severely injured.

The case was closed "not rehabilitated" with the simple note, "deceased."

Case Study 9

T. M. T.

Negro – Male – 22
High School Graduate
Single
Drug abuse characterized by an inability to adjust vocationally and socially

Referral Source Information

Thomas (Tom) was referred to the Department of Vocational Rehabilitation by the drug clinic of a hospital. He was a 22 year old Negro. His disability was drug abuse (heroin). His parents are both high school graduates. The father maintains the family on his salary. Tom is the oldest of three children. The family situation seemed to be a close, well-adjusted unit. Tom's drug problem apparently developed through peer group association during his senior year in high school.

Social Evaluation

As stated above, Tom's home environment was a good one. He started experimenting with drugs during his senior high school year as "an experiment with friends that became a habit that I could not control." Fortunately, Tom had a healthy family situation to turn to with his drug problem.

Psychological Evaluation

Tom was interviewed and given the Wide Range Achievement Test, Level II, and the Gates MacGinitie Reading Tests, Survey E, Form I. On the WRAT, he earned the following grade level scores:

Reading	7.5
Spelling	7.2
Arithmetic	7.7

As a high school graduate these scores are significantly low. He was nervous on the reading test and attempted too quickly to pronounce the words. He made mistakes that he probably would not have if he had not been so nervous. Tom also made many careless errors in arithmetic. On the whole, Tom's suspected ability is higher than that indicated by the test results.

He was polite and motivated. Tom arrived for the test promptly. Although he did not do well, he did try on each of the tests. He was nervous and obviously not feeling well, which affected his test performance. It was felt by the psychologist that Tom would have problems on vocabulary and should have some remedial or prior instruction before entering a training program.

Medical Evalution

Tom experienced the normal childhood diseases. He had an operation when twelve years old which left him with an atrophied right calf muscle. His physical limitation were: lifting, bending and marching activities. He was rejected from the service induction because of his leg. Tom checked "yes" to: difficulty with vision; loss of weight, and nervous or mental trouble. The operation on his leg was for "club foot." He felt that his weight loss was due to the intake of heroin. Height was 6′ ¾″; Weight 147 lbs.

Vocational Evaluation

Tom expressed interest in going to business school. He had no vocational history at time of referral other than a limited work experience with a telephone company.

Educational Evaluation

Tom was graduated from high school but was no real scholar. He ranked 328 in a class of 472.

Narrative

Diagnostic information was gathered on Tom. He was next involved in a program for drug rehabilitation at a local clinic. Tom was put on methadone treatment to relieve his heroin addiction. It was decided that Tom should go to business school. Since tests indicated that Tom was weak in necessary vocabulary, mathematical, and comprehension skills, he was enrolled in 20 instructional lessons in vocabulary and basic mathematics so as to prepare him for the business courses. The Department of Vocational Rehabilitation provided books, tuition and transportation. Tom did well in the courses of study and was enrolled in business school for business management study. He earned "A's" and "B's" in his first quarter of study. His progress was excellent and his methadone treatment has been cut to very low amounts. This client is well motivated and willing to realistically face his problems in a constructive manner.

Case Study 10

C. W. B.

Black – Male – 23
Married
9th Grade Education
Drug abuse characterized by an inability to adjust vocationally and socially.
Character disorder (inadequate personality)

Referral Source

Mr. B. was referred to the Department of Vocational Rehabilitation by the pre-natal clinic at City Hospital. He and his wife are currently undergoing family counseling prior to the birth of their child. He had previously been a client of DVR but was closed from a referred status for failing to respond to attempts of counseling or evaluation. He has been in the city's methadone treatment program for the last five years for his heroin addiction.

Social Data

Mr. B. is a 23 year old male. He is married and is expecting his first child. He and his nineteen year old wife are presently living with his uncle in center city. They have been drawing general relief for the last two years.

Mr. B. became addicted to heroin at the age of 14. His drug abuse began with the use of marijuana at the age of 13. He graduated to heroin and after three years his maximum usage was three bags a day. When he was thirteen, he lost his mother upon whom he was extremely dependent, and was virtually on his own. His father separated from his mother when he was very young. He remembers nothing about his father. It was at this time he began experimenting with drugs.

Mr. B. presents a pleasant, neat appearance. His dress reflects his constricted economic circumstances. His social life is quite limited, partly due to economic circumstances and his rather narrow range of interest.

Medical Data

Mr. B. stated that his health is good. While he was on drugs, he suffered from malnutrition. But since he has been on the methadone program he has regained his health.

The local physician found Mr. B. to be well developed and well nourished and in no apparent distress. He is oriented in all spheres. On the basis of the general medical examination recorded, Mr. B. seems to not have any overt physical or emotional problems. His drug seeking behavior is apparently under control by methadone.

General Medical Examination

GENERAL APPEARANCE – This is a 23 year old black male who is well developed and well nourished with no acute distress.

PULSE	78
RESPIRATION	18
BLOOD PRESSURE	115/75
SKIN AND HAIR	normal
HEAD	normal in size and shape
EYES	brown
TEETH	good
NECK	normal
SPINE	No deformity
CHEST	Lungs are clear
HEART	normal
ABDOMEN	negative
EXTREMITIES	no gross physical abnormalities
NEUROLOGICAL	no gross physical abnormalities
REFLEXES	present
WEIGHT	142 lbs.
HEIGHT	5′7″
IMPRESSIONS	This individual is in normal health

Educational Data

Mr. B. dropped out of high school after the ninth grade. He

stated that his grades while in school were average and below C's and D's. His major reason for leaving school was financial – being on his own, he felt that he needed to make some money. While in school he did not participate in any extra curricular activity. Overall, he found school to be of little interest or value to him.

Psychiatric Evaluation

The psychiatric evaluation found Mr. B. to be evasive about his psychiatric history and drug history. He presents overt psychiatric symptoms of anxiety and tenseness in normal situations. Episodes of depression were noted but were not considered extremely significant. This particular individual is characterized as having an inadequate personality. It is my impression that Mr. B. is a young man, not greatly endowed intellectually. On top of this, he is passive, inadequate, dependent, and lacking drive and energy. Certainly a training program within his limits of intellect and emotional stability is in order. However, Mr. B. should not be placed in a situation which would cause frustration. He fears failure a great deal and will take it rather badly.

I would suspect that he has developed sufficient obsessive defenses that will enable him to make a reasonably good employee once he can settle down into a semi-skilled "rut."

He has a tremendous amount invested, from an emotional point of view, in his present marriage. He will work hard to achieve stability in this situation.

Psychological Data

A battery of tests consisting of the WAIS, Graves Design Judgment Test, Minnesota Clerical Test, The Crawford Small Parts Dexterity Test, Wide Range Achievement Test, the Thurston Interest Schedule, the Incomplete Sentence Blank, Draw a Person and the Cornell Index–Form N2.

The results are indicated below:

WAIS; Norms 23 year old group

Verbal Subtest Scaled Scores

Information-7	Arithmetic-6
Similarities-9	Digit Span-9
Comprehension-6	Vocabulary-5

Performance:

Digit Symbol-12	Picture Design-6
Picture Comp.-8	Object Assembly-10
Block Design-11	

Verbal IQ--83
Performance IQ--95
Full Scale–87

Graves Design Judgment Test

raw score 56--85th percentile

Minnesota Clerical Test

raw score 149–93rd percentile

Crawford Small Parts Dexterity Test

Pins and Collar	subtest	40%
Screws	subtest	73%

Wide Range Achievement Test

Reading	3.9 grade	2%
Spelling	3.7 grade	2%
Arithmetic	4.9 grade	4%

Thurston Interest Schedule

Highest interest was the physical science, art, and business areas. Area of least interest was computational.

Mr. B. is a person in the mid-range of dull normal verbal intellectual ability and lower in the middle average on the performance scale. His full scale score places him in the upper range of dull normal intelligence. He possesses good skills in the areas of abstract reasoning and short term memory. Hampered by poor vocabulary and limited information fund, Mr. B. lacks the ability to deal with tasks requiring social knowledge.

The results of the tests indicated that he possesses adequate manual skills to function in construction areas. He would be hampered in training that required reading skills such as heavy equipment operations.

Personality

Responses on the Incomplete Sentence Blank suggests an immature young individual. He has feelings of hostility directed toward his father. He prizes work highly and is very concerned about his ability to function in competitive physical tasks. Also of great concern to him is his present unemployment situation.

The Cornell Index revealed that Mr. B. has little trouble in relating to those around him. He is troubled about unemployment which affects his feelings of adequacy and self-worth.

It is recommended that Mr. B. avoid any training programs that require a classroom situation. He could function in a on-the-job program in the construction area.

Vocational History

Mr. B. is presently unemployed. His longest period of employment was as a long shoreman. This job lasted for four years. He left because of an apparent lack of demand for his services. He then went to work for a trucking company as a packer. He left this job because of poor pay. The last job he held was as a metal cutter for a bathtub company. This job lasted for a month. He was fired because of absenteeism. Mr. B. stated that his absenteeism was due to his involvement with drugs.

Eligibility

Mr. B. functions at the dull normal intelligence level and has no salable job skills. He has been addicted to heroin and is currently under treatment for his addiction. His previous employment has been sporadic and without any skill value. His inability to obtain stable employment and support his family has caused depression and anxiety. With his inadequate personality and lack of training, he has been unable to maintain permanent employment. His frustration tolerance and self image is low. He also has difficulty in relating to authority figures. These conditions constitute an employment handicap.

Vocational Objective

CARPENTER'S HELPER – Mr. B. has had some previous

experience in carpentry handiwork and with some success. He wishes to be trained as a carpenter's helper and eventually will advance to apprentice or master carpenter.

This goal is within his capabilities, provided he is adequately prepared for the work task. In order to gain the necessary training and skills the client will have to be helped to prepare for interviews, situations and questioning by prospective union apprenticeship programs.

Plans

The client will be provided counseling and guidance and given help in preparing for apprenticeship program interviews and for training.

Case Study 11

W. D. R.

Negro – Male – 18
Single
High School Graduate
Drug abuse characterized by an inability to adjust vocationally and socially

Referral Source

Mr. Ross was referred to the Department of Vocational Rehabilitation by Dr. Davis of City Hospital, where he was seen in a drug treatment clinic. He is currently on a Methadone Program and is in the detoxication process. Due to his drug problem, he has been unable to keep a steady job.

Social History

Mr. Ross is an 18 year old Negro male. He dresses in a neat modest style and has apparently good hygiene. His family consists of his mother, who works as a clerk; his father who is a waiter in New York; two sisters – 15 years old and 17 years old living with his mother; one brother attending Howard University and another with his father in New York. Mrs. Ross apparently knows of her son's addiction. Mr. Ross's addiction created some "hassels" between his mother. There is no known history of drugs in any of the other family members.

Mr. Ross was a dealer for six months before he began experimenting with drugs. He averaged 50 to 60 dollars per day selling on the street. He began snorting heroin one and one half years ago "to see what everyone got so excited about." After a few months using this method, Mr. Ross began mainlining to obtain quicker results from heroin. During his addiction, Mr. Ross supported a big financial and pharmacological habit by dealing and hustling. His stealing, robbing, and purse snatching brought him $35-75 per day. For one year he used heroin every day. He stated that his supply was endless so he never went four hours between hits. On the streets Mr. Ross was what is termed, a "good junkie." He was good to other junkies when they needed a hit and they were good to him. Most of his friends were junkies. He presently hits 20-25 caps per day. Although he is a drug addict, he denies any serious use of drugs other than heroin. Mr. Ross has never used LSD, speed or Seconal.

Mr. Ross has never been arrested for drugs but has had a long standing history of petty thievery and minor skirmishes with police. He presents a picture of "always out for a fast buck." The attitude of Mr. Ross seems somewhat "standoffish." He expresses a desire to kick and wants a job, i.e. "good life." His past work experience indicated an inability to hold a job due to his drug habit.

Medical History

Mr. Ross stated that he has had a previous history of asthma and was seen in the City Hospital Adolescent Clinic four years ago. He was treated with desensitization injections.

The present medical problem is drug addiction. Mr. Ross has experienced some sickness with drugs i.e. abdominal cramps, rhinorrhea, nausea and vomiting. He has had no previous history of abcess or hepatitus due to drugs. Mr. Ross' general medical examination was conducted at the City Drug Treatment Clinic.

The examining physician feels that it will be a "long hard road" for Mr. Ross. It was also felt that if the client would become employed he could better handle his time while on the Methadone Program. Boredom and frustration have had addicts who had once kicked to go back to drugs. Mr. Ross has in the past weeks become bored and frustrated due to the lack of a job.

Physical Exam

GENERAL APPEARANCE	Cooperative, calm, neat
HEIGHT	6'2"
WEIGHT	192 lbs.
VISION	OD 20/200
	OS 20/200

SKIN Color	Pigmentation – Freckles, Dry
	Eruptions, acne – none
	Icterus – negative
	Pallor – negative
	Palms – dry
	Vaccination Scar – negative
	Other Scars – negative
HAIR	dry
EARS	Hearing – good
	Canals – clear
	Drums – clear
EYES	Pupils – equal
	React to light – accommodation
NOSE	Obstruction – negative
	Sinus Tenderness – negative
MOUTH AND THROAT	Oral hygiene – poor
	Gums – fair
LYMPH GLANDS	negative
THORAX	negative
LUNGS	clear
	Equal breath sounds
BLOOD PRESSURE	90/74
HEART	regular rhythm
ABDOMEN	soft
GENITALIA	negative
NEUROLOGICAL	negative
FEET	negative
POSTURE	good
HABITS	Nail Biting – negative
	Tic – negative
	Speech – negative
Masculinity or Feminity	
PERSONAL TRAITS	Confident

SYSTEMIC REVIEW

HEADACHE	"migraines"
HEARING	negative
COLDS	yes

HAY FEVER	yes
ASTHMA	desensitization
CHEST PAIN	negative
PALPITATION	negative
DYSPNEA	negative
COUGH	negative
WHEEZING	negative
APPETITE	yes
INDIGESTION	negative
ABDOMINAL PAIN	yes
NAUSEA	yes
DYSURIA	negative
FREQUENCY	negative
JOINT PAIN	negative
ATHLETIC INJURIES	negative
THUMBSUCKING	negative
BEDWETTING	negative
SLEEP	negative
DREAMS	no
EXERCISE	negative
FATIGUE EASILY	negative

POSITIVE FINDINGS (include patients need)
1. Mild Photophobia
2. Stated desire to kick

TENTATIVE DIAGNOSIS
1. History of asthma (took desensitization injections)
2. Heroin addicted (admitted)

DISPOSITION, PRESENT RECOMMENDATIONS
1. Lab work
2. Follow-up on asthma if needed
3. Urine dark (question hepatitus)

After Mr. Ross' physical examination, he was placed on 40 mg. of methadone with a urine check three times a week. Two weeks later his dose of methadone was cut to 30 mg. He was placed on a detoxification methadone treatment.

Educational History

Mr. Ross graduated from the local high school two years ago in a general program of studies. His performance in high school was below average. As the client progressed from one grade to the next, there was a deterioration in grades achieved. By his senior year, Mr. Ross had only one course grade better than a D. However, he did obtain an A in Industrial Arts. Also, between the eighth and twelfth grade, Mr. Ross' attendance decreased substantially. His tardiness increased significantly over the five years. Mr. Ross was not involved in any extra-curricular activity during his high school career. He is presently interested in training that would involve using his hands. He is especially interested in wood working and Industrial Arts.

On the SCAT given in the eleventh grade, Mr. Ross ranked in the 13 to 17 percentile on Verbal, 41 to 68 percentile on Quantitative and 30 to 42 percentile total.

Mr. Ross indicated that he liked school but felt that it "did little to train him for work."

Vocational History

Mr. Ross has had several jobs each lasting only a brief time. His first was with a local restaurant where he was a kitchen helper. He earned $1.85 per hour. This job lasted one month with Mr. Ross quitting due to his drug habit. His second job was with a large local department store. Here he was a stock clerk and earned $1.95 per hour. He was fired after two months because he missed work due to drugs. Next, Mr. Ross was employed with another local department store as a night janitor, earning $1.60 per hour. He was fired from this job after four months for the same reason, i.e. missing work due to his drug habit. His last job was as a janitor for a local insurance company where he also did some clerical filing. This job lasted for a summer at the end of which he was fired again for the same reasons.

Mr. Ross expressed a sincere desire to work. This desire was one of the major reasons for his going for treatment of his drug problem. He is tired of losing jobs because of drugs. He wants to contribute to society and receive some of the benefits of work.

He is interested in industrial arts training. He likes to fix things and "loves to work with his hands." Mr. Ross wanted to go into a job that he enjoys and feels that "this is one step toward being straight."

Psychological Data

No psychological test data was obtained for this case. From Mr. Ross' high school records along with the doctor's and rehabilitation counselor's observations, it was felt that Mr. Ross was relatively well adjusted. He did become bored and frustrated during the initial methadone treatment program due to idleness. He does need support and guidance in facilitating better use of his time.

Initial Services

Due to Mr. Ross' need for immediate job placement a more permanent vocational objective was planned after Mr. Ross was temporarily employed. Several employers were contacted and Mr. Ross was employed with Town Auto Parts as a stock clerk. He was paid $2.50 per hour. He still expressed an interest in wood working. He investigated the wood working courses at City Technical School and was interested in the cabinet making course. After this visit Mr. Ross quit his job and dropped out of sight. Several attempts were made to contact him but all were fruitless. After almost two months, he showed up at the rehabilitation counselor's office. He stated he had gone back into the streets dealing and occasionally was using heroin. About three weeks ago he decided that he did not want this type of life, and went back on the methadone program. He realized he had made a mistake and this time he was going to stay off heroin.

Mr. Ross was then sent to Youth Opportunities and to City Hospital to inquire about a job. Later that day Mr. Ross returned informing the rehabilitation counselor that he had secured a position in the transportation department at City Hospital. The idea of attending the City Technical School cabinet making course was discussed. Rehabilitation would pay for the first session and if he kept his job, he could pay for the second semester.

Rehabilitation Plan

Mr. Ross was certified eligible for rehabilitation services. His disability was diagnosed as drug misuse characterized by an inability to adjust socially and vocationally. There was no secondary disability.

The vocational objective was determined as cabinet maker. Mr. Ross is now clean of drugs and is maintaining himself through the Methadone Program at City Hospital. Since he is able to maintain himself, it was felt that he is ready for training and employment. He enjoys working with wood, and is interested in learning how to make cabinets. It was felt that this vocational objective was reasonable for this client, because it was in the line with his interest, abilities, and aptitudes. With the methadone treatment, continued medical services from the drug clinic and extended guidance, counseling and follow-up, there is a reasonable expectation that Mr. Ross will be able to maintain himself in training and employment.

Summary of Services

The client continued to be seen by the Drug Treatment Center for guidance and counseling. He received guidance, counseling and related follow-up services from and at no cost to Department of Vocational Rehabilitation. Job placement services were provided, and the client has secured a position in the transportation department at City Hospital. Due to the fact that this is a probationary status employment, the Department of Vocational Rehabilitation sponsored his first semester of night training so that he could stabilize himself financially. The estimated duration of services was one year.

Overall Cost and Plans for Financing

To: City Technical Center
2020 Westwood Avenue
Cabinet making course – one semester – $30.00

All other services will be provided at no cost to the Department of Vocational Rehabilitation.

Summary

Mr. Ross was seen on the job several times by the rehabilitation counselor. He reported that his methadone continues to be lowered. He was earning $1.70 per hour but recently received a raise to $2.30 per hour. Mr. Ross likes his present employment but stated he is continuing in his cabinet making course, by paying for the semester at City Technical School.

What Mr. Ross stated about his school training was found to be untrue. A representative of City Technical School called the rehabilitation counselor and informed him that Mr. Ross attended only the first two sessions of the course. The client was then confronted with these facts. Mr. Ross said he did not want to tell the counselor that he had not been keeping up with "everything." He also stated that he would like to continue with his present employment. He had received a raise and he had a good chance to keep increasing in pay. He felt that he was treated well by his employers and his co-workers.

Mr. Ross was then closed "rehabilitated" with the vocation of transportation worker.

Case Study 12

R. E. M.

Male – 21
Single
10th Grade Education
Inadequate personality with paranoid tendencies due to drug intoxication

Referral Source

Mr. M. was referred to the Veteran Hospital (VA) by his parents, who were very concerned about their son's drug addiction. Mr. M. began using drugs while in the Army and continued to use drugs since his discharge, two months ago. He has previously lost a job as a salesman with a major tire company, which may or may not be related to drugs. Mr. M. says he realizes the fatal prognosis and wants to get off drugs so he can go to work and make a fresh start.

Social Data

Mr. M. is a 21 year old man who was admitted to a VA Hospital for drug misuse. His parents are a very pleasant and neatly attired couple. His father is in his early forties, his mother is in her late thirties. He was their first child. There are six other children in the family. The parents describe Mr. M's early childhood as a very emotional one. He had temper tantrums frequently and often passed out from crying so hard that caused him to quit breathing. During his adolescent and teenage years he was always quiet and had only a few friends. He also never has been too comfortable with girls. His parents made a point of saying that he did not run around with the "hell raisers" and seemed to think that this was one of the biggest points in his favor. Although he uses drugs, Mr. and Mrs. M. feel their son is not a bad boy.

Mr. M's parents related some of their son's guilt feelings over problems with their younger son, Jim. It seems Jim ran away from home just two days before Mr. M. returned home from the service.

Jim ran away with a 35 year old woman who Mr. and Mrs. M. feel was manipulating and using him.

He now feels that Jim ran away because of him, although he had been quite close to his younger brother. Jim is still away from the home although his parents have heard that he is well. There are six siblings in the family, sisters aged 18, 14, 8, and 5, and brothers aged 16 and 11. Mr. M. comes from a family that is described as comfortable with the necessities of life but never an over abundance of money. His father works regularly and is very strongly committed to the value of work; "the necessity for hard work to get any where in life." His mother is a warm supportative person who is greatly distressed over her son's use of drugs and weeps easily on discussing this.

Both parents claim that they knew nothing of his taking drugs until recently when they first noticed a gross change in the patient's behavior. They described him as being normal, outgoing, and happy when he first came home and then overnight he became very depressed and very frightened. Mr. M's rapid decompensation was followed by:

1. paranoid feelings in regards to people in the back yard laughing at him;
2. attempts made by neighbors to harm his family physically and their reputation;
3. his reluctance to get off the bus when he was going down town to the employment office which caused him to stay on the bus the entire route and just go right back home and stay in the house, totally afraid to leave the house.

At this point, Mr. M. and his parents felt the need for hospitalization and very anxiously presented himself to the VA office.

He dropped out of school in the tenth grade because he was in constant trouble with the teachers. He enlisted in the Army, thinking that the Army life would be so nice. When he was disappointed and frustrated in the Army, he began taking drugs in order to relieve his depression while in Korea. He was taking speed, grass, and LSD. He had thirty trips on LSD in the last two years. Mr. M. a Vietnam veteran, was discharged from the Army with a general discharge under honorable conditions. According to

Mr. M's information he continued to take drugs until one week prior to being admitted to the VA Hospital.

His girl friend left him because he was on drugs but now because he sought treatment, she has returned to him.

Educational History

Mr. M. completed 10 years of school and was described as an average student. He did not participate in extracurricular activites in school. He did enjoy playing basketball around the house but never played it in school. Once he got into high school he could not adjust to the high school routine. His parents were not really sure what it was, if it was that he could not grasp the material or if the classes were too competitive with the other students. During his stay in the VA Hospital, Mr. M. took and passed his General Educational Development (GED) test.

Psychological Data

Mr. M. was referred for psychological evaluation in order to assess possible organic impairment caused by his drug usage. He was administered a battery of tests consisting of the Wechsler Adult Intelligence Test, Bender-*Gestalt,* Projective Drawings and the Rorschach.

Test Behavior

Mr. M. was cooperative, coherant, and relevant throughout the interview and testing. He manifested some interest in and motivation to succeed in the tasks. The major clinical impression of this young man was that of a beaten individual. Although Mr. M. was quiet, soft-spoken and self-denigrating generally, there were occasional sparks of animation.

Test Findings

The measure related to intellectual functioning suggest that this veteran has not suffered organic impairment due to the drug use.

His Full Scale IQ on the WAIS was 105 indicating that he is currently functioning in the normal range. (Verbal IQ – 106, Performance IQ – 103) While Mr. M. seems to have the potential for bright normal functioning there are indications that emotional and environmental factors have interferred with his developing adequately. He performs well on tasks that require nonverbal skills, demonstrating moderately above average ability to concentrate and attend freely to noninterpersonal tasks. His performance decreases on the more academic, verbal, and interpersonal tasks.

Mr. M's performance on the projective measures indicates some of the likely sources of his emotional and intellectual difficulties. These are quite consistant with the veteran's description of his family relationships and his schooling.

He has apparently employed denial as a major defense against strong feelings of inadequacy. These inadequate feelings seem to stem from the relationship Mr. M. had with his father. His father is seen as a strong masculine figure who apparently thought little of his son and at least unconsciously made that quite clear. Unable to deal with these feelings and resolve this relationship, Mr. M., as he entered adolescence, apparently took the "easy way out." "If I am nothing, I'll flunk out of school, etc.," at the same time he was a "man" in this flunking subgroup.

Mr. M. appears to be basically bright and a sensitive young man. He seems aware of the raw deal he dealt himself in order to cope with his emotional stress. This has apparently heightened his feelings of inadequacy and lack of self worth and through the denial there is a fairly strong feeling of depression. In efforts to combat these unacceptable feelings of inadequacy Mr. M. at times comes across as hostile and aggressive. This dynamic picture may help to explain his choice of "Uppers" rather than "Downers" or any other drugs.

At the present time Mr. M's use of denial is sufficiently intact to interfere with his adequately grappling with, and resolving these inter and intrapersonal difficulties himself. It is the clinical psychologist's opinion that, if Mr. M. is, or can be, motivated enough to enter into individual psychotherapy or intensive counseling, he has the capacity for insight and growth. Additionally, when such counseling is undertaken, Mr. M. seems quite capable of furthering his education vocationally, and perhaps, even academically.

Summary

Mr. M's current performance indicates that he is in the normal range of intellectual functioning. There is no evidence in the protocol to suggest organic impairment or psychosis. At the present time he may be considered an inadequate personality with paranoid tendencies due to drug intoxication. The records suggests that attitudes within his family have fostered this self perception. Therapy could prove beneficial and is recommended.

Medical History

Mr. M. has a history of drug usage which led to his military discharge and subsequent admission to the VA Hospital. He has been hearing voices and is panicked that someone is going to hurt him, although he does not know who this someone is.

Mr. M's mental and physical status reveal an 18 year old male, thin, looking utterly panicked, eyes red from tears, claiming he does not trust anybody and is afraid to be in the building because "the whole world is crazy."

Mr. M. states that he has been in good general health except for these feelings. Smoking, occasionally drinking, and use of LSD, speed, and marijuana are Mr. M's habits. He has had none of the childhood or adult illnesses and is sensitive to poison oak.

Because he is afraid, Mr. M. claims that "they" think he is a queer, and an addict, and so on . . . The physician felt that the client was inadequate, immature, and withdrawn, with a flat affect.

Physical Examination

Patient is in no distress, well oriented.

EYES	negative
THROAT	negative
NECK	no adenopathy

LUNGS	clear to A and P
HEART	negative
ABDOMEN	soft, no masses, no area of tenderness
REFLEXES	patellar – o.k.
DIAGNOSIS	acute psychosis, paranoid type

Vocational History
Testing & Counseling

Prior to enlisting in the Army Mr. M. worked as an inspector for nine months at D & H, a screw machine company in his home town. After his discharge from the army, he worked for a major tire company as a salesman. Mr. M. lost this job due to his drug misuse.

A battery of vocational and interest tests consisting of the Lee Thorpe Occupational Interest Inventory, Minnesota Vocational Interest Inventory, and the Edwards Personal Preference Schedule were administered by a counseling psychologist. According to the Lee Thorpe Occupational Interest Inventory, Mr. M. showed interest in the mechanical field, and he would be satisfied in being an electronic pressman, or a stock clerk. He also stated that he would like to be trained as a steam fitter.

According to the Edwards Personal Preference Schedule, he sees himself as being an aggressive, exhibiting, showing off person. However, according to our observation, and other test findings, he is an immature, meek, fragile, and not too adequate person. In reality, he is only 18. He could be given some allowance to be immature. We are only glad that he now realizes that he can get along so much better without the effect of drugs.

Mr. James Smith, Mr. M's former employer at D & H, was approached about Mr. M's re-employment. Information was made concerning Mr. M's re-employment with D &H Company, upon Mr. M's release from the hospital.

Hospital Summary

Mr. M. on admission was markedly frightened and suspicious.

He stated that the whole world looked crazy to him. On the admission ward, he presented himself as a hostile and negative person. He requested his discharge against medical advice. After being coaxed by the staff, he opened his mind and admitted his paranoid feelings and suicidal ideas. While in the hospital Mr. M. continued to suffer from ideas of reference and persecution for quite awhile. He is uncooperative and angry, claiming that he was not sick. A urine test proved that he was not taking his medication. He was confronted about this and he agreed to take his medication provided that it would not make him drowsy. Mellaril, 50 mg. q.i.d., was prescribed. Once this medication was increased, Mr. M's condition began to improve.

Mr. M. has shown quite a bit of improvement in his condition since being admitted. His affect now seems more appropriate and he is showing more spontaneity. He seems free from psychosis but could have flash backs in the future from his past experiments with LSD. Mr. M. has been on several passes home and has apparently refrained from taking drugs while there. The hospital staff feels that Mr. M. is ready to go back and resume working as an inspector at D & H Company. This will place him back in a familiar place where he feels he is wanted. And, he knows too where to go and what to do when he is ready for the GI bill training as a steam fitter. He also agreed with us that he will seek supportive therapy and counseling at a mental hygiene clinic. Upon discharge Mr. M. was given a 21 day supply of Mellaril.

Case Study 13

S. T. K.

White – Male – 24
Single
High School Graduate
Drug abuse characterized by an inability to adjust vocationally and socially

Referral Source

Mr. K. was referred to the Department of Vocational Rehabilitation by the Halfway House drug treatment center. He was referred because at one time he was addicted to heroin. A secondary disability of diabetes was also noted. In addition to his treatment for drug addiction, he has also been receiving treatment through the city hospital diabetic clinic.

Social Data

Mr. K. is a 24 year old male. He was born July 22, 1949 in this city, the second oldest of four children in his father's second marriage. His father also had nine children in a prior marriage. His father is 70 years old. He completed the seventh grade. He is presently a retired employee of the S. Paper Company, however he does part time carpentry work. Mr. K's mother was a house wife most of her life, however, she died in 1968 from diabetes.

Mr. K. stated that he began using drugs seven years ago at the age of 15. He first began with marijuana. Three years later he began using heroin. He became addicted, using 14 capsules per day. Mr. K. stated that he finally realized that his addiction would ruin his life so he voluntarily entered the Halfway House drug treatment center. In his spare time, Mr. K. enjoys reading books, particularly those concerning sociology. He also dates, plays basketball and football.

Medical Data

He has suffered from the usual childhood diseases, and stated that his present health is good. However, he does suffer from diabetes. This requires him to take a daily shot of insulin, NPH insulin-80 units per day. His mother died of diabetes at the age of 49. Mr. K. is being treated at city clinic for his diabetes.

He formerly used a number of drugs including marijuana, cocaine, and heroin. At one time he shot 20-25 pills per day to sustain his habit. However, he related that he has not used drugs of any kind for over a year.

GENERAL MEDICAL EXAMINATION:

HEIGHT	6′2″	
WEIGHT	201 lbs.	
EYES	normal	20/20 both eyes
EARS	normal	
NOSE	normal	
MOUTH	extensive decay of teeth	
THROAT	normal	
NECK	normal	
LUNGS	no evidence of disease	
HEART	normal	
BLOOD PRESSURE	120/72	
PULSE RATE	76	
EDEMA	none	
ABDOMEN	normal	
NERVOUS SYSTEM	normal	
SKIN	clear	
FEET	normal	
ORTHOPEDIC IMPAIRMENTS	none	

Mr. K. is in good general health with the exception of his diabetic condition.

Educational Data

Mr. K. graduated from City High School in June of 1967. He then went to a small college in North Carolina in September of the same year. He remained there until 1970 when he withdrew a week before the final exams. He returned there briefly in the summer session but did not receive any credits, as he again withdrew. He has a "C" average and lacks only four hours of being classified a senior. He stated that after he got diabetes, he lost his scholarship in football and was unable to finance college any longer.

Vocational Data

Mr. K. has been principally employed in summer jobs. In the summer of 1967, the subject worked at City Hospital. His duties were those of a porter, and he earned $50 per week. His ability on the job was described as poor, and he is not eligible to be rehired.

He worked the next summer for the month of August at the City Pharmacy. His duties were those of a delivery boy and miscellaneous worker, and he earned approximately $158.00 during his brief employment. The subject related that he quit his job to return to college.

His next employment was from June until August at E. G. Engineering. He worked as a laborer on the night shift. He quit this job according to the records to take a better job, however, he related that he left to return to college.

He related also that he was a member of the Staff for a few months during his stay at Halfway House. A staff member in his position was paid $5500.00 per year. He lost this job, when he quit the Halfway House temporarily in June of that year.

Most of the jobs Mr. K. has had were just summer jobs, with the exception of the Halfway House.

Treatment Data

Mr. K. entered voluntarily into the drug treatment center in January of 1971. After six months he made staff and was involved in counseling. He then dropped out for several days and when he returned he was placed in resident status. He remained until December, 1971. He was transferred to out-patient care. The final report indicates:

Overall level of motivation	excellent
Attitudes and Involvement	excellent
Utilization of Services	excellent

Positive relationships with peers	excellent
Self discipline	excellent
Responsibility	excellent
Initiative	excellent

Mr. K. has developed into a dynamic, strong character. His earnest efforts are felt amongst the staff and residents. He portrays "role model" traits as a striking example of what can be accomplished by sheer determination and will power.

In the final stages of Mr. K's out-patient care counseling Mr. K. revealed interest in becoming a drug addiction specialist. It is felt that this vocation is appropriate for Mr. K's ability and interest. He was then referred to the Department of Vocational Rehabilitation.

Vocational Objective

DRUG ADDICTION SPECIALIST – This vocation fits Mr. K's interest and abilities. It is felt by the staff of the treatment center that he has the insight and can function in this capacity. This vocational objective is within the capability of Mr. K.

Case Study 14

R. G. L.

Black – Female – 21
Single
High School Graduate (Two Years College)
Drug abuse characterized by an inability to adjust vocationally and socially. Character disorder with aggressive and infantile manifestations.

Referral Source

Miss L's initial referral to vocational rehabilitation was by Dr. Wood of the drug addiction clinic of City Hospital where she was a patient from an overdose attempt. The referral was made for purposes of counseling and support. Miss L has been unable to adjust due to drug abuse. Drug misuse has handicapped Miss L both educationally and vocationally. At the time of the suicide attempt it was felt that further treatment was needed and presently it would be unfeasible for Miss L. to receive vocational rehabilitation services. Miss L. was later referred by Mr. Trice of a local drug treatment program.

Social History

Miss L. is a twenty-one year old, single, black, female from the Bronx, New York. She has a three year history of heroin abuse along with a potpourri of other drugs including cocaine, barbiturates, LSD and methadone. She graduated from Thomas Jefferson High School in New York where she was in the top quarter of her class. After graduation, she came to this city and attended City University for two years before dropping out and going back to New York.

Both of Miss L's parents are living and other significant family members include her older sister, Carol, who lives in Washington and her younger sister, Joan, a graduate of a local drug treatment program and currently a staff member.

Miss L. was recently detoxified from heroin addiction in New

York via Methadone. She then came to this city to visit her sister. On the third day of her visit, she left her sister's home in an apparent daze. She was later found by her sister walking the street in a confused and disorganized state. Miss L. entered her sister's car and within five minutes had a major motor seizure. She was brought to the Emergency Room with a history of having taken 10 to 12 grams of Isoniazid in a suicide attempt. In the Emergency Room, she had four more major seizures, poorly controlled with ten milligrams i.v. Valium doses.

Miss L. was first introduced to drugs while a senior in high school. She stated that her reasons for using drugs was to become part of the "in" crowd at school. Her first experience was with soft drugs (marijuana). She gradually progressed to LSD and finally heroin.

Medical History

Miss L. stated that she has been in generally good health since she detoxified from heroin in New York. There is no history of hepatitus or abcess due to her drug use. Physical examination at the time of Miss L's suicide attempt revealed a well-developed, well-nourished, black female who was agitated, tachypneic, but awake and responding to commands. Her blood pressure was 140/90; pulse 98, temperature 101.3; respirations-28. The pupils were equal and reactive to light. The examination of the heart showed a normal sinus rhythm without murmurs or gallops at a rate of 95 beats per minute. The Neurological examination was given. Miss L. responded to commands and appeared to realize what was going on about her. Her sensory and motor systems were intact. No pathological reflexes were present. She had hyperactive deep tendon reflexes bilaterally. No muscle weakness was evident.

Thirty-six hours after ingestion, the patient was awake and oriented, breathing normally off the nasal oxygen with normal vital signs. At the time of discharge, the patient was alert and oriented.

DISCHARGE DIAGNOSES:
1. Isoniazid toxicity
2. Seizures secondary to #1
3. Metabolic acidosis secondary to #1, resolved

DISPOSITION:	1. Appointment in medical follow-up clinic at which time a lateral chest will be done.
	2. Appointment in the psychiatry clinic.

Physical examination was given after client recovered from her overdose.

General Medical Examination Record.

R. G. L.	Age 21 Female Single
HEIGHT	5′5″
WEIGHT	105 lbs.
EYES	Normal – Conals
EARS	Hearing good
NOSE	Normal
MOUTH	Normal
THROAT	Normal
LUNGS	Chest films show no evidence of aspiration pneumonia
ABDOMEN	Normal
SCLERAE	Not icteric
CIRCULATORY SYSTEM	Normal
NERVOUS SYSTEM	Normal
SKIN	Clear and normal
ORTHOPEDIC IMPAIRMENT	None
LABORATORY DATA	Blood gases on the Bennett respirator showed a PO2 of 108, pCO2–25, ph 7.20 and a bicarbonate of 9. Blood sugar – 199 White blood count was 16, 900 Sodium – 150 Potassium – 4.2 Chloride – 102 CO2 – 12

	Chest films revealed a right hilar density with no evidence of pneumonia.
EXTREMITIES	No cyanoses, clubbing, or edema Good peripheral pulses

Educational History

Miss L. graduated in the top quarter of her class at school. While there she was especially interested in the arts, i.e. music and painting. She did not participate in extra curricula activities. She stated that she was a "loner" and had few friends. There was no indication that school authorities knew of her drug addiction.

After graduation from high school, Miss L. came to this city and attended City University for two years. This was due in part to her sister living here. Her curriculum area was liberal arts with emphasis in music. During her two college years, she became more involved with drugs especially heroin. Her grades began to drop and Miss L. finally withdrew after her second year and went back to New York.

Vocational Data

Miss L's work experience has been limited to the summer months between school years. Her principal employment for her summers was as a waitress for a nationally known restaurant chain. This job was temporary in nature. The client has no interest in this area as far as permanent employment is concerned.

Psychological Data

Due to her suicide attempt, Miss L. was referred for psychiatric evaluation. The report stated that this client has no prior history of overt psychiatric systems. Over the past two weeks, Miss L. has had suicidal ruminations, insomnia, sadness or crying. She describes her life as one of loneliness and sadness. She indicated that she was unable to form close relationships with others. It was also felt by the psychiatrist that Miss L had occasional blurring of ability to organize thinking. With this mild uncontrolled thinking, her affect is flattened. She denied depressive systems at present.

Miss L's history suggests early signs of schizophrenia. The possibility exists that the central nervous system stimulating inclination of the Isoniazid may be exposing an otherwise subclinical thought disorder.

When Miss L. was asked to reconstruct the night of the suicidal attempt, she was unable to remember any of the night's experiences. She stated that when she recovered from the effects of the drug, she did not realize why she was in the hospital.

Miss L. was seen as an above average person in general ability. The fact that she was a good student in school is indicative of her ability. It was felt that she could best benefit from an intensive drug treatment program. In such a program support and counseling could provide her with the needed tools enabling her to make an adequate adjustment. She will also be provided with constant supervision. The rehabilitation counselor concurred with these recommendations. Due to drug addiction and misuse, she has been functionally limited in that she has been unable to adjust socially and vocationally. In order to learn to live free of drugs in our society, she became an in-patient at a local drug halfway house. It was the opinion of the rehabilitation counselor that Miss L's disabling condition presented a definite vocational handicap in that she was unable to maintain herself in society, unable to continue in college and unable to obtain and maintain employment.

The final clinical impression was that she had a definite character disorder with aggressive and infantile manifestations.

Report From The Drug Treatment Center

Upon first entering the program, Miss L displayed an over-evaluation of herself in terms of an attitude of superiority. She was condescending, arrogant, uncooperative and cynical. She listened to no one and chronically alienated others around her. It was felt that this infantile behavior was a manifestation of severe feelings of inadequacy. She exhibited a rather cavalier attitude toward her own life when she first entered the program. One week prior to coming in as a program participant she attempted suicide by taking a large number of Isoniazid tablets. When talking to her about this she reacts with unrealistic good humor as if it were some kind of a joke.

After not being able to be handled well in several of the local drug facilities, she was assigned to the North Street Halfway House where she finally responded. The staff members began to see the development of positive attitudes in relationships with others, a friendliness and a development of a definite warmth which was not present before. She also accepts criticism without becoming antagonistic and hostile.

Her improvement was to such a point that it was felt she could stabilize in a work situation. There has not been, on the other hand, a complete resolution of the conflicts she brought with her upon entering the program. With positive support, she has responded greatly and if this is continued in the program and on the job, more growth can be expected. Miss L's vocational rehabilitation counselor was notified as to her improvement and her readiness for work.

Eligibility

Miss L's primary disability has been diagnosed as drug abuse characterized by an inability to adjust vocationally and socially. A character disorder characterized by aggressive and infantile behavior has been diagnosed as the secondary disability. Due to drug addiction, she has been functionally limited in that she has been unable to adjust socially and vocationally. In order for her to live free of drugs in our society, it was necessary for her to become an in-patient at a drug treatment halfway house. It is felt that through the services and support of the drug treatment program, this client will be rendered fixed to return to gainful employment.

Plan and Summary

A rehabilitation plan was written with detective (undercover operator) as the vocational objective. This vocational objective was felt to be reasonable and attainable in that this client is well qualified based on her varied drug experience to work in undercover work to help in identifying drug abusers. This position will be an on-the-job training situation in which she will receive training and experience as a nurses' aide as well as working as an undercover agent.

Summary of Services

Miss L. will enter an on-the-job training situation at no cost to DVR. She will receive the necessary uniforms and transportation needed to begin this employment. She will also receive follow-up services to assure satisfactory adjustment to the job. While involved in the training and employment, she will continue as a halfway house resident where she will receive continued treatment and support. The estimated length of services is four months.
Total Cost to DVR $58.50.

Case Study 15

B. T. S.

White – Male – 19
Single
High School Graduate
Drug abuse characterized by an inability to adjust vocationally and socially

Referral Source

Mr. S. is a 19 year old white male. Two years ago, this client was in a vocational rehabilitation school unit. During his senior year he dropped out of school and left town. He has recently returned to Richmond and was referred to this vocational rehabilitation counselor by his former school unit counselor as a client in need of services due to residuals of drug addiction.

Social History

Mr. S. comes from a disrupted family background. This client's mother died when he was very young and he was raised and cared for by various women within the family (2 sisters and an aunt). The client remembers being extremely effeminate and afraid of his peers. His father has been a disabled alcoholic for a long period of time. Mr. S. had interrupted relationships with his father and received no financial support or guidance while growing up. The client stated that he separated completely from his father when he was fifteen years old. Ever since he has been on his own, searching for his identity and attempting to cope with his emotional problems.

Mr. S. has been a drug user since his high school years. This client was a heavy user of amphetamines and eventually became dependant upon these drugs. He has also used LSD and speed. His leaving high school during his senior year was due primarily to drug abuse. After Mr. S. dropped out of school, he went to Canada, gradually worked his way across the states and finally became a "speed freak" in San Francisco's Haight Ashbury. He lived with a couple and their child. During his stay in Haight Ashbury, Mr. S. was seen by a psychiatrist in a Free Clinic where he was found to be an extremely depressed youth with homosexual drives and a drug dependancy, (see psychological). He was placed in a drug treatment center and withdrew from drug use.

Mr. S. is a seemingly bright young man who is attempting to work out his problems and his loneliness without family guidance and support. He has been living with friends and acquaintances for the past two years. He is seen by the vocational rehabilitation counselor as cooperative, alert, and quite willing to bend to survive.

Educational History

Mr. S. completed eleven and one half years of school before dropping out and going to San Francisco. While there he did manage to finish his remaining course work and graduated from a local San Francisco high school. Also while in California, Mr. S. qualified for civil service by passing the Civil Service Examination. He is an intelligent individual who expresses a desire to go to college or to learn a skill or trade.

Vocational History

Mr. S's vocational experiences are limited due to his home environment, drug abuse, and age. He never has worked while living in this city. While in San Francisco he did qualify and passed the Civil Service Examination. He then secured a job with the postal department as a clerk in the concentration center. He earned three dollars per hour. He held this job for two weeks before he was forced to quit due to drugs. This client managed to find odd jobs and eventually worked his way back to this city. He has since been unemployed receiving support from his friends and relatives.

Psychological Data

Psychiatric Abstract From the Haight Ashbury Free Clinic

Mr. S. presents symptoms of anxiety and depression. He is a highly dependant youth and has been placed in a situation with which he is unable to cope – following a failure of a mother substitute relationship. He has been clinging to this relationship for some time as a defense against his very strong homosexual drives. However, he has recently entered into a homosexual relationship with another young man, and as a consequence feels that he has achieved some resolution of his identity conflicts.

This client has been a drug user for many years and has recently become dependant upon amphethamines. It is quite probable that his present emotional state is in part due to wasting effects of continued use of amphetamines, LSD and other psychedelic drugs.

In summary, Mr. S. has an inability to function in the appropriate musculine roles and has resolved his psychosexual conflict through a homosexual adjustment.

Since data was not obtained in regard to Mr. S's school cummulative record, the Revised Beta and the Kuder Preference Test were administered by the vocational rehabilitation counselor. The Revised Beta revealed a score of 120 placing Mr S. in the upper limits of average intelligence. The Kuder Preference Test indicated this client's interests are in the fields of literature and art.

These findings were discussed with Mr. S. He stated he has done considerable writing of poetry and prose and apparently has talents in those areas. Mr. S. intends to further develop these talents in college. But, at the present time he strongly wants to become self supporting preferably through sales or clerical work. These are his stated goals at the present.

Medical History

Mr. S's medical history reveals that he has had no systematic difficulties or apparent illness except the residuals of drug abuse. Mr. S. was sent to a local physician for his general medical examination. On the basis of the following report no further recommendations were made.

General Basic Medical Examination Record

FREQUENT HEADACHES	no
HEARING	no
EXTREME FATIGUE	yes
NERVOUS SYSTEM	normal
PERSISTENT COUGH	no
PAIN IN CHEST	no
UNUSUAL IRRITABILITY	yes
SWOLLEN ANKLES	no
LOSS OF APPETITE	no
DIFFICULTY IN MEMORY	no
TB	no
HERNIA	no
OPERATION	no
HEMORRHOID	no
DIARRHEA OR CONSTIPATION	no
EYES	20/20 – left 20/20 – right
NOSE THORAX	negative
LYMPHATIC	normal
HEART AND CIRCULATION	normal
ABDOMEN	normal
ANO-RECTAL	normal
DIFFICULT VISION	yes
FAINTING	no
ASTHMA	no
UNUSUAL GAIN OR LOSS OF WEIGHT	no
COUGH PRODUCING BLOOD	no
SHORT BREATH	no
FEVER	no
DIFFICULTY IN THINKING	no
FREQUENT INDIGESTION	no
RHEUMATISM	no
CONVULSIONS	no
VARICOSE VEINS	no
ACCIDENT	no
BURNING IN URINE	no

HEIGHT	73″
WEIGHT	129 lbs.
HEARING	o.k.
MOUTH OR TEETH	normal
CHEST & LUNGS	normal
BP	100/50
GENITO-URINARY SYSTEM	normal
SKIN	normal

Eligibility

Mr. S's primary disability has been diagnosed as an emotional disorder characterized by an inability to stabilize in work. A secondary disability has been diagnosed as residuals to drug abuse. Mr. Smith expects to later complete his education in college but at this time he needs to gain his independence and self esteem. Because of his exceptional talents intellectually and his personal insights into his problems along with his withdrawal from drugs usage, there is reasonable expectation that he can be gainfully employed.

Plan

A vocational plan was written with sales clerk as the vocational objective. This vocational choice was based on the client's intellectual ability, experiences, and interests. It was felt by the counselor and the client that time was needed for the client to plan his future. A stock clerk position was found with a local department store. The client will earn $50/week.

Services Rendered

Guidance and Counseling
General Medical Examination
Transportation
Rent for a month
Food bills for a month
Clothing

Job Placement
Follow-up

Cost to Vocational Rehabilitation – $250.00
Client was closed; rehabilitated

Case Reopened

Six months later, Mr. S. came and told his rehabilitation counselor he quit his job after six weeks. The position as a stock clerk was not challenging enough for Mr. S. He stated that he needed to be more deeply involved in some occupation more in line with his self image.

Mr. S. appeared to be hostile, depressed and lonely to the vocational rehabilitation counselor. He blurted out his feelings in a somewhat philosophical manner. He spoke of moving many times in the past six months. He wanted to talk about the state of the economy and he didn't believe there was a job "out there for him." He has been disappointed in not getting a job as a mail clerk.

His Kuder Preference Record Vocational (KPRV) was again interpreted for him. Some effort was made to explore which move would be more in the direction of his long range goals.

"Library Assistant" and "Proofreader" seemed appropriate jobs for consideration. Local opportunities might include copy editing with a newspaper. Literary and musical interest of a quite professional caliber were also suggested by the KPRV. Mr. S's intelligence supports this. An appointment was made for Mr. S. to take the General Aptitude Test Battery (GATB), which will possibly confirm his musical mastery.

It was felt that Mr. S. may have real potential as a composer and arranger if he is willing to go through formal training. At this time he frowns upon formal education and wants to get a job. He doesn't feel academic discipline is that important since he picks up things very quickly on his own, including some composing of music.

GATB scores indicate Mr. S. is capable in most areas:

G – 133	N – 130
U – 145	S – 107

P – 121	F – 106
Q – 154	M – 91
K – 140	

Mr. S. was informed of the results. The conversation tended to center around music as his long range area of interest. He has considered music school. The vocational rehabilitation counselor stressed the importance of some concrete long range planning and the use of his talents. An appointment was made with the chairman of the music department of City University.

Mr. S. would first like to work in the Post Office to prove to himself that he can hold a job for at least one half year. An appointment was made with the Post Office about a job as a clerk.

In his interview with the chairman of the music department, Mr. S. played some of his original compositions. The chairman felt Mr. S. has good potential in the area of music and persuaded him to apply for admission as a music student.

Mr. S. then talked to the personnel director at the Post Office concerning employment. He trimmed his hair and presented a neat appearance for the interview. He mentioned his prior use of drugs to the personnel director. The vocational rehabilitation counselor felt this probably killed any chances of him getting a job.

The client was then urged to search for jobs in the city. He found a job in a medical lab and was hired by Dr. Hane. Mr. S. discussed the possibility of on-the-job training as a lab assistant under Dr. Hane's direction. It is a thirteen month training program.

Mr. S's GATB reveals that for the vocational profile of the Medical Lab Assistant, he has more than sufficient scores to qualify him for this work (Requirements G-110, S-95; P-110; Client has G-133; S-107; and P-121).

The Kuder Performance Test did show a correlation of 79 percent in scientific computation and the clerical field. He is well motivated to pursue this goal having had discussed this with Dr. Hane of the Department of Anatomy – under whom he will be working. This program offers ample opportunities for future employment since a local hospital expects to hire all of these trainees. The client will learn to dissect and prepare specimens for slides and to do all the jobs related there to and to operate completely with full responsibilities as a medical lab assistant. Tuition will be payable to the Department of Anatomy for this training at a rate of $86/month. Maintainance to be sought through the Department of Public Welfare and the Training Services Project at a rehabilitation center.

Total Cost of Services $2,318

Dr. Hane will be supervising training and totally responsible for all of Mr. S's weekly hours, progress and reporting to the counselor.

Job duties:

1. Learn the preparation of tissue and various techniques.
2. How to assist in surgical operation of animals.
3. Learning the ordering and caring of equipment.
4. Learning the care and treatment of animals for research.
5. Learn to use all equipment.
6. Learn the proper method of mixing and using stain chemicals and dyes.

Mr. S. received a Training Service Project stipend with the stipulation that the money will not be paid if the student has:

1. Three absences in a week
2. Placed on leave for more than one week
3. Progress is unsatisfactory
4. If client leaves training program

Client entered the training program in April. After the first month, Mr. S. was doing a moderately good job. Dr. Hane felt his main problem was that of being easily offended by any types of critical opinion related to work. Mr. S. knows the techniques on paper but occasionally has a little trouble transposing this knowledge to practices. He attempts to do some things without really thinking carefully about them before doing the task. Dr. Hane has stressed the importance of his appearance and communications with his fellow workers.

The vocational rehabilitation counselor feels that the client is having difficulty in regulating himself to work and in personal regimentation but is making progress and is "sticking with it."

Several months later, Mr. S. was again evaluated. Dr. Hane indicated that Mr. S. is learning the proper skills well and does a good job when told what to do. Dr. Hane senses a feeling of importance to the functioning of the Lab by Mr. S. Progress is being made both in technical skills and fellow relationships. The vocational rehabilitation counselor counselled his client about his appearance. He accepted this and changed it sufficiently.

In the last progress report received, Dr. Hane indicated Mr. S. is increasing in skill proficiency. Client is still having trouble in the area of seeing what is to be done. He misses things that should be done without being told. The rehabilitation counselor felt Mr. S. was improving in this motivation, acceptance of responsibility and initiative. He has come a long way from "wandering in the streets."

During the fourth month of on-the-job training, Mr. S. began experiencing peculiar sensations which he described very vividly as "drifting away or being unassociated with reality." He is also aware of occasional hallucinatory experiences especially of visual and especially when looking at a blank wall or into a clear sky.

Mr. S. was sent to Dr. Owens, a neurologist. In addition to the above sensations the client has had on occasion some olfactory hallucinations with varying and different odors each time. He denies headaches, depotopia tenitius and peripheral paratheseas. The neurological examination is entirely within normal limits except for a very slight difficulty walking a tandem.

The EEG is abnormal showing some spontaneous paroxysmal dysrhythmic slowing occurring at frequent intervals lasting 1 to 3 sec. These changes are consistent with this symptomatology and as his history might suggest. It is difficult to know the etiology of this abnormal EEG. It is likely that this is a residual of some recurrent toxia or anoxic cerebral manifestations occurring in the past.

INTERPRETATION: Paroxysmal dysrhythmic slowing. This change suggests a diffuse corticoil dysfunction of a chronic nature and the possibility of a lowered seizure threshold to generalize non-convulsive and/or convulsive seizures without aura. These recommendations and changes should be improved with Valium.

Summary

After six months in the training program Mr. S. terminated himself by leaving and going on the "road" again. It was felt by the rehabilitation counselor that the client had begun to take drugs again.

Vocational Rehabilitation could not accept him for services again unless he went to a drug treatment half-way house for therapy. He refused to do this. This case was then closed in Status 28 – reason – failure to cooperate.

Case Reopened

After a month, Mr. S. contacted his vocational rehabilitation counselor and asked for drug therapy and a chance to continue in his training. After a month in a drug treatment half-way house, client left. The vocational rehabilitation counselor was unable to locate Mr. S. This case was closed in Status 08.

NOTE: The vocational rehabilitation counselor last heard that Mr. S. is in Belgium traveling from place to place.

Case Study 16

D. A. L.

White – Male – 24
Divorced
High School Graduate
Schizophrenic reaction, paranoid type with a diagnosis of drug addiction

Referral Source Information

Daniel is a Navy veteran with a history of drug abuse and schizophrenic reaction, paranoid type. He was transferred from a Naval Hospital in Ohio to the Veteran's Administration Hospital there. He is presently in a civilian mental hospital with a diagnosis of drug addiction and schizophrenic reaction, paranoid type. He is Caucasian and 24 years of age.

Social Evaluation

Daniel's parents have been divorced since he was five. He has one younger brother. The younger brother is also a drug abuser. His mother has a history of instability. The father is a lawyer who spent some time in jail for bad check writing. A millionaire grandfather left money in a trust for Daniel when he reaches 40. Daniel was married, but information on his wife is not available. Now Daniel is divorced.

Psychological Evaluation

Daniel has a history of assault charges in the service and as a civilian. While jogging one day he came across two grave diggers and maliciously beat them. He was arrested for that incident. He was diagnosed in the civilian hospital as schizophrenic, paranoid type. Daniel claimed he had been Jesus Christ for a while and later thought he was Joe Namath. His delusional preoccupations were also present during his Naval career. He is also aggressive and combative. His affect was labile and his mood anxious. He admitted to auditory and visual hallucinations. Insight and judgment were only fair.

On the ward Daniel was a constant agitator of other patients, also with nursing and ward personnel.

Gradually Daniel began to show improvement in his condition. He became more cooperative and manageable. He was given an industrial therapy assignment and ground parole privileges. Daniel did well on the industrial assignment. He was allowed a weekend pass to visit his fiancé. Subsequently he was put in an open ward.

Medical Evaluation

Daniel is within normal physical health. He did evidence hypochondrical beliefs during the examination. He thought that he had asthma and a peptic ulcer. Tests were negative. His left eye was twitching. From past fights he had a history of cracked ribs, busted hands, and shackle sores.

Vocational Information

Daniel was a sonar technician in the Navy. After the Navy experience he worked as a technical representative for sound systems.

Educational Evaluation

Daniel is a high school graduate. He was trained by the Navy as a sonar technician.

Narrative

On admission to the hospital this client was diagnosed as having schizophrenic reaction, paranoid type. He had auditory and visual hallucinations. He also had delusions about being Jesus Christ, Joe Namath, and a fish. He progressed, during 20 weeks of daily group therapy, from a closed ward to industrial work assignments, ground parole privileges and weekend passes. He is still progressing and will hopefully be transferred from an in-patient status to an out-patient status.

Case Study 17

C. A. B.

White – Male – 26
Single
College Graduate
Drug abuse characterized by an inability to adjust vocationally and socially

Referral Source

Calvin is a 26 year old, Caucasian, male referred by a local hospital. His disability, as reported, was drug addiction and inability to adjust socially or vocationally. He was diagnosed as being addicted to heroin since Summer 1968.

Social History

This client has had trouble stabilizing himself in work or school since drug addiction. He moved from a very rural setting to the "big city" to go to college. Calvin felt inadequate to cope with the complexities and animosities of "big city" life. So, he turned to drugs and ultimately a drug sub-culture. He dealt in drugs for many months, selling and dispensing drugs and equipment. Finally, he was forced to withdraw from college. Afterwards he took himself to Canada on a self-cure trip. Miraculously he attained his goal. Later he referred himself to the Adolescent Clinic of a hospital for counseling.

The client's mother and father are separated. He has two sisters, one older and one younger; also, two brothers, one older and one younger.

Psychological Data

Calvin was referred for psychological assessment to determine feasibility and eligibility for vocational rehabilitation services. He had taken no drugs for two years and hoped to complete his course work toward a degree in sociology. After that he hoped to teach high school English in a rural setting. Later, he hoped to join the Teacher Corps.

The following tests were used in the evaluation:

Bender–*Gestalt*
Wechsler Adult Intelligence Scale
Draw-A-Person
Thematic Apperception Test
Minnesota Multiphasic Personality Inventory
California Personality Inventory
Mooney Problem Check List

Calvin arrived for testing appearing generally unkempt. He approached the tests matter-of-factly and sincerely. He was thoughtful before responding and indicated when he was guessing. The evaluator reported him as a pleasant person to work with.

Calvin's performance placed him in the bright-normal range of intellectual functioning. All scores were in average limits or slightly above. Most elevated were scores on information, vocabulary, and comprehension. This probably reflected his past intellectual achievement. He has sufficient intellectual ability to continue academically. Calvin also had somewhat above average ability to synthesize and abstract new materials. He was most lacking in numerical ability. There was also a minimum impairment of eye-hand coordination.

Calvin's personality assessment indicated that he was a guarded individual. The MMPI indicated that Calvin was a passive, dependent person with feminine interests. In addition, latent if not overt homosexuality was indicated. On the Mooney he cited "being too inhibited in sex matters" as problematic, and Card 13 MF of the TAT elicited a theme of a "man failing after trying to prove his maleness." Another card elicited the theme of a young man being seduced by an older man.

It was conjectured that the sexual conflict indicated was related to his perceiving females as authoritarian and rejecting. His mother was of this sort. Calvin stated that he would like to marry; "however, his affective ties with his mother and past experience may be sufficiently negative to prevent him from approaching females." Other cards indicated thought control by unconscious influences – possibly his mother.

Calvin seemed fearful of the future but had sufficient social skills and his interpersonal values were sufficiently integrated to allow him to function effectively and responsibly.

In summary, Calvin had homosexual conflicts resulting in problems, e.g. impotence and latent homosexuality, in close heterosexual relationships. Conflicts with his parents were unresolved. He was passive and dependent. On the positive side he did have well enough integrated values and social skills sufficient enough to allow him to act responsibly. He was intellectually able to finish college course work. Since he intended to teach high school English, it was recommended that he receive psychotherapy concurrently with his academic work.

Medical History

Calvin did not have useful binocular vision due to a handicap arising from exoptropia. With strabismus surgery it was corrected somewhat. Besides that his vision was poor but correctible by glasses.

He had contracted serum hepatitis while in the drug sub-culture. It was recommended that he be put on a multi-vitamin, high protein, low fat diet.

Vocational History

Calvin's vocational objective was teaching. Before becoming involved in the "drug sub-culture" he had worked part-time and received a State Educational Assistance Authority loan. Due to drugs and hepatitis he finally was forced to withdraw from college. He went to Canada on a self-cure which worked and was treated for hepatitis by the referring hospital. With the aid of vocational rehabilitation he has been able to finish his course work and get a degree. He is now teaching in a rural setting.

Educational History

Calvin started out in education in college then switched to sociology after becoming involved with campus protest and concern with national and international iniquities. As indicated above he dropped out due to drugs and hepatitis. He, as indicated above, is now a teacher. He plans to eventually get a master's degree and join the Teacher Corps.

Narrative

Calvin was referred as a drug addiction problem who was unable to adjust socially or vocationally. He was cured of hepatitis and freed from drugs. He made an exceptional withdrawal from heroin. The prognosis for rehabilitating this client was excellent. He was alert, well qualified and anxious to complete vocational college training.

Calvin has been employed for over a year now as a teacher. He has been closed out as successfully rehabilitated. The services provided were: psychological evaluation, tuition to college for completion for one-half year, maintenance, transportation, methadone, hospitalization for strabismus surgery, guidance, counseling, and later follow-up.

Case Study 18

C. L. C.

White – Male – 27
Divorced
11th Grade Education
Passive aggressive personality with drug dependency and hypochondriacal neurosis

Referral Source

Clyde was referred to the Department of Vocational Rehabilitation with a disability listed on the referral form as hepatitis. He was just out of a home designed to help drug users. In the home ex-drug addicts acted as models and a source of support for drug addicts. It was a live-in situation. Clyde was a 27 year old, divorced, Caucasian male.

Social Evaluation

Clyde was "hooked" on drugs through experimentation with his peer group. It was not until he was 25 years old that his father discovered that he was an addict. His father then committed him to a mental institution. Clyde escaped from the institution and went back to the street and to drugs. After a year he committed himself to the "home" and was rehabilitated. He still suffers from the effects of drug addiction but is "off" drugs.

Psychological Evaluation

It was found in the psychological evaluation that Clyde was sensitive and rather intelligent. Many of his problems, past and present, were due to personality inconsistencies. Although he was off drugs, he was still suffering from their effects and this was most certainly impairing his ability to deal with his present day problems. Clyde evidenced a strongly dependent and very effeminate personality. This was causing many of his problems. The final diagnosis was "passive aggressive personality with drug dependency and hypochondrial neurosis."

Clyde was evaluated for achievement level with the Adult Basic Learning Examination (ABLE) to ascertain his readiness for acquiring his GED equivalent. The results of the ABLE are listed below:

Vocabulary	9.0+
Reading	9.0+
Spelling	9.0+
Arithmetic Computation	5.6
Arithmetic Problem Solving	7.0
Arithmetic Total	6.1

The evaluator felt that Clyde was well enough motivated to acquire a high school equivalency diploma. Clyde was excited at the GED idea. He said that he was willing to try anything to keep his mind busy and keep him off the streets.

At this point Clyde opened up with the Counselor. Clyde felt that he had found someone that would not castigate him because of his problem. He felt that the counselor trusted him and treated him as an equal. Clyde discussed his drug problem. He just as many others experimented with marijuana and "hard" drugs. He talked about his forced commitment by his father and subsequent escape.

Clyde was never maintained on methadone. With the aid of the home for drug addicts he "kicked" the habit. This really shows his sincere commitment and realistic approach to his problem.

Medical Information

HEIGHT	5′11¼″
WEIGHT	174 lbs.
NOSE	right side obstruction
VISION	20/20 corrected.

Normal childhood diseases.

Vocational Information

Clyde has had only factory experience as a laborer. He showed very little direction in employment interests just setting the arbitrary condition that the pay be about $3 an hour.

Educational Information

Clyde finished the 11th grade before dropping out of school.

Narrative

Clyde's disability was defined as drug abuse (heroin). The psychologist further diagnosed him as having a "passive aggressive personality with drug dependency and hypochondriacal neurosis." Clyde showed high motivation toward earning a high school equivalency certificate. He was enrolled in a GED preparatory program. He expresses interest in continuing his education past the high school level. The counselor believes that Clyde will do well with his obvious high motivation and sufficient ability.

Case Study 19

A. S. C.

White – Female – 17
Single
10th Grade Education
Inability to adjust socially and vocationally characterized by drug abuse

Referral Source

Ann was referred to the Department of Vocational Rehabilitation by the guidance counselor of a local high school. She was sent because of her acting out behavior, drug involvement, and truancy. She and her mother were finally brought before the assistant principal and she was given an indefinite suspension. She was later withdrawn permanently upon the recommendation of the school administration.

Social Data

Ann is a seventeen-year-old single, white female who presently lives with her divorced mother and younger fourteen year old sister. She presents a mod, attractive appearance. She has long black hair and overall is a very pretty girl. Ann stated that she and her sister relate well and have the same outlook on various subjects. Her mother has been divorced for five years and has supported her family as an executive secretary for a large industrial company in the city. Ann, according to her mother, has been a problem child. She has had problems in adjusting to school since her early elementary grades. When in her early teens she became promiscuous and began using drugs, particularly marijuana and LSD. During her fourteenth year she was arrested four times. Three of these arrests were for running away and living with older teenagers. The other arrest was for possession of marijuana. All charges were dropped. When approached concerning this behavior, she stated that "she knew it was wrong but couldn't say no to her friends." This apparently accounts for her truancy at school in that she would be easily persuaded to absent herself from school or leave during the school day.

Ann has no steady boyfriend as she "likes to play the field." She calmly spoke of her intimate encounters as if a mark of success. Her mother has had considerable problems over Ann's promiscuity. Boys will call up at all hours asking for Ann. The calling progressed to the point that Ann's mother had to acquire an unlisted number.

Ann is interested in reading and music. She stated that she could listen to music all day. She likes to "hang around with other teenagers especially those that are involved in meaningful movements." She wishes that she could leave home for good and feels her mother is forcing her to be someone she is not.

Medical History

Ann has had the normal childhood diseases. She informed the counselor that she feels that she is in good physical health. A physical examination was requested by the rehabilitation counselor.

PHYSICAL EXAMINATION

HEIGHT	5′4″
WEIGHT	110 lbs.
EYES AND VISION	normal
EARS AND HEARING	normal
NOSE, THROAT, AND NECK	normal
MOUTH AND TEETH	normal
LYMPHATIC SYSTEM	normal
CHEST AND LUNGS	normal
HEART AND CIRCULATORY SYSTEM	normal
BLOOD PRESSURE	110/70
ABDOMEN–HERNIA	normal
GENITO - URINARY SYSTEM	normal
ANO-RECTAL	normal
NERVOUS SYSTEM	normal
ENDOCRINE SYSTEM	normal
SKIN	good
VARICOSE VEINS	negative

SKELETAL OR ORTHOPEDIC	normal
Present limitation as to work capacity	none
Types of activity to be avoided	none

Educational Data

Ann was withdrawn from high school after completing the tenth grade. Her school grades indicate a better than average student. She had maintained A's and B's throughout her educational experience.

However, her academic performance in school was marred by a behavior characterized by an inability to adjust to authority, truancy, verbal abuse to teachers and a general inability to adjust to the stresses of school. Several attempts by school officials to provide a less stressful school environment failed. She was suspended several times in her final year in school. In the final week of her tenth grade she and her mother were called to a conference with the principal and counselors of her school. It was recommended by the school officials that Ann be permanently withdrawn from school. She was then referred to the Department of Vocational Rehabilitation by the visiting teacher.

Vocational Data

Ann has never had any job experience. She finds this not creditable for a girl of her age. Her interests are in the secretarial and receptionist fields.

Psychological Data

She was sent for psychological evaluation by the rehabilitation counselor. The WAIS and the Bender-*Gestalt* were given.

TEST RESULTS AND OBSERVATIONS:

Throughout the testing session, Ann was extremely anxious and at times suspicious of the examiner. Rapport was established readily, although it was felt that Ann was not comfortable during the session.

On the verbal portion of the WAIS, she attained a verbal IQ of 116, ranking at a bright normal level of intelligence. Interest scatter was minimal although intra-test scatter was more evident. Her poorest performance was on tasks requiring the recall of general information, an active relationship with her environment, and passive attention to verbal stimuli. Her best performances were on tasks requiring adequate judgment in the formation of verbal concepts. On the performance section of the scale, she achieved a non-verbal IQ of 104, ranking at an average level of intelligence. Inter-test scatter was more pronounced here than on the verbal section. Her poorest performance was on a task requiring visual motor coordination of an imitative type. Her best performance was on tasks requiring the ability to discriminate the essential from non-essential elements of a situation and perceptual motor abilities of a reproductive nature. On a scale as a whole, Ann achieved an overall IQ of 112, ranking at a good, bright-normal level of intelligence. The scatter pattern of subtest performance, however, suggests that emotional factors may have been serving to interfere with her performance. It is essential that her performance on the non-verbal section of the scale is a better estimate of her innate intellectual ability.

The results of the Bender-*Gestalt* Test do not indicate the presence of any significant amount of organic brain damage. The *Gestalten* for the most part are well reproduced but do contain distortions usually associated with emotional disturbance. In this respect, the Bender-*Gestalt* protocol substantiates the suggestions of the WAIS. Ann's self-concept is of an individual of high average intelligence. This is a realistic estimate of her current level of functioning. She perceives her mother as rating her much brighter and this may reflect demands made upon her by her mother. At the present time, Ann is unsure of herself and expresses a desire to "straighten" herself out before going back to school. She believes that she has emotional problems and verbalizes a desire for professional help. In light of data contained in the test protocols as well as material from the interview, it is felt that Ann does have significant emotional problems and it is suggested that she receive a more complete psychological evaluation in order to better determine the extent and nature of her problems.

Before the evaluation for eligibility was completed, Ann was committed to a mental hospital by her mother. Her case was then closed by the counselor.

Case Study 20

J. G. S.

White – Female – 18
Single
High School Graduate
Character disorder (inadequate personality)

Referral Source

Miss Scott was referred to Vocational Rehabilitation by Dr. Wilson of the City Hospital Adolescent Clinic. Miss Scott has had a long history of adjustment problems and has a severe drug problem. She is presently on 35 mg. of methadone per day.

Social History

Miss Scott is an 18 year old white female who has graduated from high school. She lives with her father, mother, sister and three brothers. Her father is employed as a mechanical engineer at Philip Morris and her mother works at St. Mary's Hospital as a medication technician.

She is a very attractive adolescent who has been on and off heroin, LSD and marijuana since she was 14 years old. At age 16 she was a self referral to Dr. Wilson's Adolescent Clinic with the chief complaint being overweight and dysmenorrhea. Upon evaluation, she was referred to a psychologist who found she had a severe drug problem. From medical and psychological results it was felt that while she was treated for her medical problems, she should also be referred to a psychiatric social worker.

The social worker saw Miss Scott and her family once a week for the next two years. During this time, she went through several traumatic experiences. The first was a friend's suicide resulting from an overdose of LSD. Some weeks later, a girl friend's father tried to seduce her. These two factors plus her own identity problem created an adjustment reaction with severe depression. During this period of depression she began living with her boyfriend who was also a heavy user of drugs and who was increasingly turning her on to heroin. Also at this time the family involvement with her psychiatric social worker became strained due to a disagreement between the father and the social worker. The social worker then contacted Dr. Wilson to inform him of present events.

Finally, Miss Scott was arrested on drug charges and placed in a detention home. From a conference with Dr. Wilson, the parents, lawyer, and the rehabilitation counselor, it was felt she would benefit from vocational rehabilitation and a methadone program with supportative therapy. With these facts in mind, Miss Scott was released from the detention home.

Miss Scott started taking drugs because "she thought her peers were boring doing childish things and she found herself hanging out with older people who turned her on to speed, and then other drugs."

The family situation is strained. Miss Scott states that she gets along with her mother as long as they do not talk about emotionally charged subjects. She feels her mother does not know how to relate to many of the things that she was experiencing. She does not get along with her father and 16 year old sister but has a good relationship with her three younger brothers. Her concern is that her parents are inconsistent with her younger brothers as they were with her. She worries about her sibling's reaction as they get older.

Psychological Evaluation

On May 18, 1971, Miss Scott was referred by Mr. Moore of the Department of Vocational Rehabilitation to Dr. Silvers for a psychological evaluation.

The client was seen by the psychologist as an attractive older adolescent who was candid and cooperative throughout both the interview and test. She readily answered most of the examiner's questions as long as the questions dealt with purely factual material. When questioned about emotionally charged material, she answered perfunctorily, but one time cried, became very angry, and would not further discuss the topic. When asked what being drug free meant to her, she was unable to address herself to this question and at this point cried. She admitted that she could not guarantee that she would not go back to heroin.

Evaluative Procedures

Wechsler Adult Intelligence Scale
Rorschach Technique
Thematic Apperception Test
Bender *Gestalt* Reproductions
Sentence Completion Test
Informal Projectives
Human Figure Drawings

Objective Results

128 – Verbal 125 – Performance 128 – Full Scale

Miss Scott earned IQ's on the WAIS which placed her in the superior range of intelligence. In the verbal area her highest score was on social comprehension and judgement. In the performance area her highest score was on the ability to construct familiar objects from their component parts. In the verbal area her lowest score was on the ability to do abstract reasoning. It was felt that the obtained results were both representative of her present level of functioning and optimal for her at this time. No signs of organic brain dysfunction were noted.

Miss Scott saw herself as a very angry young woman who was relatively ineffectual in her ability to express her feelings constructively. She felt strongly that she was not allowed a place in her life to use her intellectual resources but instead found herself punished for being intelligent and assertive. At present, she saw no possibility for a change in this attitude among the people with whom she had contact, and saw herself as returning to heroin as an escape from these perceived pressures. Her primary response at present was depression and being fatalistic about life.

In general Miss Scott was a very immature, dependent, anxious adolescent who felt very inadequate and insecure as a person. Her social relationships were marked by flightiness and difficulty in forming close give-and-take relationships. She feared close relationships with other people and put emotional distance between herself and all others by emotionally withdrawing from them and isolating all feelings which she might have for other people.

She wanted to live away from her parents' home as she saw herself as controlled in all that she did. At the same time, she had little idea of how to care for herself in a mature way and had little ability to form mature interpersonal relationships. Her feelings toward her father were conflictural as she saw him as punishing and at the same time, as promising emotional support to her. She almost completely denied the existence of her mother and no emotional alliance with her mother could be seen from the present information.

Overtly, Miss Scott was somewhat guarded, mildly negativistic, and highly manipulative. Covertly, her major defenses were fantasy, rationalization, some intellectualization, and repression. When faced with some emotionally threatening situation she had the ability to intellectualize and isolate all the affective charge of the situation. At the same time, she occasionally chose to respond to situations in an entirely impulsive fashion without at all thinking about the consequences of her behavior.

In summary, Miss Scott was an adolescent of superior intelligence who saw herself as inadequate and insecure as a person and presented herself as an anxious, very immature, dependent young woman. She apparently had resorted to drug abuse in an attempt to gain some feeling of her own identity. She felt that any attempt to be herself and to use her intelligence was met with consistant punishment. She feared close emotional relationships and was likely to act out impulsively without considering the consequences of her behavior. In terms of helping her develop a more positive self image, it is possible that she might benefit from a residential therapeutic community experience.

Medical History

A medical abstract received from City Hospital reported that Miss Scott was overweight and at the age of 10 began to experience dysmenorrhea. Services were provided by City Hospital in the form of medication, physical therapy, exercise schedules and guidance concerning food intake. By the time of referral to vocational rehabilitation, Miss Scott's weight and menstrual problems were under control. Miss Scott has experienced two "bombers" while on LSD and this disturbed her emotionally. The only serious medical problem from drug abuse Miss Scott has experienced is bronchitis resulting from a large amount of smoking marijuana. She has had no history of abcess or hepatitis due to drugs.

PHYSICAL EXAMINATION	City Hospital
GENERAL APPEARANCE	Pleasant
HEIGHT	63″
WEIGHT	137½ lbs.
VISION	without glasses OD 20/200
	OS 20/200
	OU 20/200
SKIN	Oily
	Eruptions, Acne mild
	Icterus – no
	Pallor – no
	Palms – dry
	Hair – dry
EARS	Hearing – normal
	Canals – normal
	Drums – normal
EYES	Pupils: Equal – normal
	React to light – normal
	Extraocular Movements – normal
	Conjunctivae – normal
	Exophthalmus – normal
	Fundi – normal
NOSE	Obstruction – no
	Sinus – Tenderness – no
MOUTH AND THROAT	Oral hygiene – good
THORAX	normal
LUNGS	clear
BLOOD PRESSURE	(recumbent): 130/70
HEART	normal
ABDOMEN	normal

GENITALIA	normal
NEUROLOGICAL	normal
FEET	normal
POSTURE	normal
POSITIVE FINDING	Mildly Overweight
LAB	CBC
	VA
TENTATIVE DIAGNOSIS	Obesity, mildly due to excessive intake

Educational History

Miss Scott graduated from a local high school where her performance was in the B and C range. It was felt by the school that she could have done better if she had tried. Miss Scott enjoyed school to some degree and was interested in art and English. Her other interests include psychedelic music, nature and arts and crafts. She does not like sports. If it is possible for her to go to college she would major either in the area dealing with work in the field of parks and recreation or in arts and crafts.

Vocational History

Miss Scott's previous work experience is limited. She has had only one job which consisted of operating the concessions at a local theatre during the summer. She earned $1.25 per hour.

Miss Scott first stated interest in arts and crafts. She has since mentioned several other areas of interest. These include social work, teaching, occupational therapy and possibly some type of job with Virginia Parks and Recreation.

Eligibility

Miss Scott's primary disability has been diagnosed as drug misuse characterized by inability to adjust socially and vocationally. She is eligible mentally, physically, and, financially for services of the Department of Vocational Rehabilitation. She is currently seeing Dr. Wilson at the Adolescent Clinic and he is optimistic about her rehabilitation. Dr. Wilson feels that with methadone maintenance and supportative counseling, guidance and therapy, this client can become a contributing member of society. DVR and Mr. Moore are in complete agreement with Dr. Wilson. Psychological, intelligence and aptitude tests also indicate that she is a capable individual. She enjoys art and hopes to take Art Education in college so she can become an instructor. Since this objective was in keeping with the client's aptitudes, abilities, interests, educational background and previous experience, it was felt that DVR services were justified.

Services

This client will continue to be seen and treated by Dr. Wilson of the Adolescent Clinic for extensive guidance, counseling and related follow-up services at no cost to DVR. Along with the Methadone Maintenance Program and tuition sponsorship for college, DVR will offer supportive follow-up services in order to insure satisfactory placement and rehabilitation services.

COST AND PLANS FOR FINANCING

Eligibility based on need. The following was authorized:

To City Hospital Methadone Program:
90 days Methadone at $1.50 day $135.00
To City University:
9 hours tuition at $19/hour 171.00
To City University Bookstore:
Books and Supplies 35.00
To Miss Scott:
12 weeks of food allowance at $20/week 240.00
ADDITIONAL SERVICES:
To psychologist:
30 therapy sessions at $30/each 900.00

Summary and Follow-up

Miss Scott left her home environment as recommended by Dr. Wilson of the Adolescent Clinic, Dr. Silvers, Clinical Psychologist, and Mr. Moore her Rehabilitation Counselor, to attend Summer School, in preparation for the fall semester (This was authorized by DVR).

The following is a record of her performance at City College:

Principles of Art – C

Nonloom Techniques – C

Composition and Literature – Incomplete

After summer school, Miss Scott was seen for an interpretative interview of the psychological evaluation which was administered prior to entering school. She concurred with most of the findings of the evaluation. Several therapeutic alternatives were mentioned including a half-way house out-patient facility, and out-patient psychotherapy with a professional.

She did not feel that she could cope with the stresses of a half-way house either on an in-patient or an out-patient basis. She also seemingly did not give too much consideration to entering psychotherapy on an out-patient basis.

A month later, Miss Scott was admitted to City Hospital due to extreme emotional problems. This plus her inability to cope with the stresses of life necessitated her to be hospitalized on the psychiatric ward at City Hospital. Her parents hospital insurance covers the hospital cost but not Dr. Silvers' fees, who has been seeing her in therapy.

After fifteen sessions of individual psychotherapy, Miss Scott's progress was slow, due to her lack of trust. Although progress regarding the sources of her problems has been slow, she has begun to show some positive practical behaviors regarding her future life. These behaviors have taken the form of asking to be withdrawn from methadone and permission to begin looking for a job.

It was felt that Miss Scott needed to continue with her hospitalization and psychotherapy. Fifteen additional psychotherapy sessions were then authorized.

Miss Scott has continued her courses of treatment on the psychiatric ward of the City Hospital and has made considerable progress. Her relationship with her therapist has developed to a point of trust and she is beginning to work through some of her problems. Presently, she has been working on the practical aspect of relating to others and on her disposition upon leaving the hospital. She has recently been talking about getting a job at a drug store and living with her grandmother or getting a room in a boarding house until she can find a more suitable job and living quarters. These thoughts appear to be quite realistic and are being supported.

After the second set of 15 sessions which were authorized, Miss Scott is still in need of continued psychotherapy. It is apparent, at this point, that any psychotherapy endeavor with her will be of relatively longterm nature, however, once she leaves the hospital, the frequency of therapy sessions will be considerably less than while she is an in-patient. She is making significant progress and is an excellent candidate for continued support by the Department of Vocational Rehabilitation.

Therapy continued with Miss Scott on an intensive basis until she was discharged and placed on an out-patient schedule. It was felt by Dr. Silvers that Miss Scott had all the necessary tools to function outside of a sheltered environment. Her future was discussed and she said that she did not want to go back to school. She also stated that she has a continued craving for heroin. This is not unusual as many ex-heroin addicts have this symptom after detoxification.

Miss Scott left for California for a vacation. She felt this would enable her to think out the best course for her future. Mr. Moore, her rehabilitation counselor, placed Miss Scott in status 24, services interrupted.

Case Study 21

F. R. J

White – Male – 27
Married
High School Graduate
Drug abuse characterized by an inability to adjust vocationally and socially with resultant physical complications

Referral Source

Mr. J. was referred to the Department of Vocational Rehabilitation by the Halfway House drug treatment center. He is currently in the resident program at Halfway House where he will remain for an indefinite period of time. Since entering the Halfway House eight months ago, he has been drug free.

Social Data

Mr. J. is a 27 year old male. He comes from a very limited urban socioeconomic background. He was the youngest of two boys. His father is a 57 year old native of this city. He is presently employed as a lab technician at a VA hospital and has been so employed for the past 27 years. His father has a high school education and is a regular member of a Baptist church. His mother is 58 years old and is also a native of this city. Mr. J's mother has a high school education and has been a housewife since her marriage. Both parents are reported in good health. His 24 year old brother is in the Army, stationed in California.

Mr. J. has been married to his 22 year old wife for two years. She is presently employed as a receptionist for the local telephone company. They have one child, a boy three years old. Mr. J. advised that they have had a happy marriage together and that his drug problem has not completely destroyed the family or the marriage. He feels his wife is staying with him.

In talking to Mrs. J. she stated that she is not interested in her husband. She feels that when he gets out of this trouble, he will do the same thing again. He has caused her a great deal of problems;

she is constantly having bill collectors around and was almost fired at her job. She does not want to have anything to do with him in the future and that she is still in the process of paying off his bad checks. She is planning on getting a divorce. She feels that she is doing quite well by herself. Mr. J. has been involved in criminal activity because of his drug habit. He was arrested twice for cashing worthless checks but he was released because of the plaintiff's unwillingness to prosecute (*Nolle Prosses*). He stated that the money was used to support his habit. More recently, he was charged with possession of heroin and was found guilty as charged. The indictment stated that he did unlawfully and feloniously have in his possession a certain, to wit: heroin, a controlled drug against the peace and dignity of the stated.

Detectives of the vice division state that they received a telephone call that a party would be in a 1968 Cougar in the area of Q Street. The detectives responded to the call and saw the Cougar in front of the pool hall, known for its illicit drug traffic. There were two men in the car and leaning on the car was a young lady who is known as a drug addict. The detective asked the two subjects to get out of the car and to show some identification. The detectives then went to the subject's car and observed a Marlboro cigarette package lying next to the door. Opening it, they observed several foil packets containing white powder. Another cigarette package was found near the first. After finding the two packages the subject was placed under arrest and advised of his rights. He was frisked and then taken to the vice division headquarters. Once there he was told to empty his pockets on top of one of the chairs. In Mr. J's pockets was a foil packet containing a white powdered substance. The drug chemist with the State Board of Pharmacy reported that the one sealed brown envelop containing one metal foil containing a white powder responded positively to the qualitative test for heroin, diacetylmorphine, a Schedule 1 drug.

Mr. J. entered the United States Navy and served two years and received an honorable discharge. While in the Navy, he served as a hospital corpsman and was stationed in Norfolk, Virginia.

The drug treatment Halfway House was notified of Mr. J. and his addiction. They stated that if the court suspends the sentence they will take him into the program. The court released Mr. J. to the halfway house. Mr. J. stated that his overall health is good. He also said that he smokes and drinks heavily. His drug abuse began six years ago when he began using marijuana and heroin. Two years after he began using heroin he was addicted. During his peak, the largest amount of heroin he needed was 15 to 20 pills a day. At the time of his arrest he stated that he was using about three or four pills a day and that he had been cutting down on his own.

General Medical Examination

HEIGHT	5′11″
WEIGHT	181 lbs.
EYES	normal
EARS	normal
NOSE	normal
MOUTH	normal
THROAT	normal
NECK	normal
LUNGS	clear
HEART	normal
B.P.	120/80
PULSE	78
EDEMA	none
ABDOMEN	normal
NERVOUS SYSTEM	normal when under medication
SKIN	clear
FEET	normal
LAB TEST	Showed elevated total protein, albumin, which is indicative of a liver deterioration
IMPRESSIONS	Deteriorated liver due to drug condition

Educational Data

Mr. J. is a high school graduate. At the time of his arrest, he was a second year freshman of City University. He was working for a degree in elementary education. His support came from his G. I. Bill. His grades at City University were poor – D's and F's. Mr. J. felt his poor performance was due to his drug habit.

Vocational Data

Mr. J. was last employed by theological schools as a teacher's aide until his employment was terminated because of the possession of drugs. He earned approximately $470 a month. His supervising teacher stated that he did a fair job when he was present but that he was absent quite a bit. She also stated that he was supposed to work, as a teacher's aide and go to school. She indicated that he took advantage of this situation. She said that she often saw Mr. J. out on the street when he was supposed to be working.

Eligibility

This 27 year old young man has been involved with drugs for six years. He has experimented with most of the illegal drugs, including heroin, cocaine and hallucinogenics. Since entering the Halfway House drug treatment program he has been drug free. Prior to his entering Halfway House he was charged with possession of heroin; and at the time of the court hearing, the sentence was suspended on the condition that he enter the Halfway House program. For the past six years, he has been functioning on a marginal basis, both socially and vocationally. Although he has held employment from time to time, he lost these positions due to his involvement in the drug scene. He has some liver deterioration, but is otherwise in good physical health. In view of his drug abuse and negative life style, Mr. J. has been unable to function adequately. With continued therapy under the halfway house program and with additional training, it is believed that this young man can become a productive member of society.

Vocational Objective

URBAN SOCIOLOGIST – This young man is a high school

graduate, who has a few credits toward a college degree. He is highly motivated at this time to pursue the above vocational objective and it is believed that he has the necessary personality and aptitude to perform capably in this area. Once training is secured and with continued therapy under the program, it is believed that he can become gainfully employed in an appropriate agency.

Summary of Services

Guidance, counseling, and diagnostic evaluation have been provided Mr. J. He is currently in the resident program at Halfway House, where he will remain for an indefinite period of time. DVR will provide approximately three years of college, tuition, including activity fees and books. It may also be necessary to provide clothing as needed for his training program. Frequent contacts will be maintained with the staff at Halfway House, as well as with client's probation officer. Once training is completed, client will be aided in securing appropriate employment in the city. Follow-up contacts will be maintained as long as deemed necessary. It is estimated that DVR services will be needed for approximately three and one half years.

OVERALL COSTS AND FINANCING:

Tuition @ $255.00 per semester for two semesters	$510.00
Activity fee @ $15.00 per semester for two semesters . . .	30.00
Books @ $50.00 per semester for two semesters	100.00

Case Study 22

D. L. L.

White – Male – 19
Single
10th Grade Education
Drug abuse characterized by an inability to adjust vocationally and socially (Heroin addiction)

Referral Source

Delbert was a nineteen year old white male referred by the adolescent clinic of a hospital. His disability was reported as "adolescent adjustment problem characterized by drug abuse." He was a diagnosed heroin addict. He had tried to quit the habit by himself but failed. Delbert referred himself to the hospital, and showed an honest desire to quit heroin.

Social Evaluation

Up to the time that Delbert referred himself to the adolescent clinic his parents knew about the marijuana usage but not heroin. This was understandable, since he was not living at home.

Delbert was a high school dropout, having completed only the tenth grade. The jobs he could get were inadequate to support his habit. So, he had resorted to stealing. Delbert has been arrested four or five times for various offenses: trespassing, disturbing the peace, breaking and entering, forgery, and car theft. He recently spent two months in jail while awaiting trial for forgery; charges were dropped.

Delbert has problems at home but mostly blames himself for this. He dropped out of school and left home because he "just wasn't getting along." The mother does not work. The father is a draftsman. Delbert claimed that he had no communication with his parents. They were more like neighboring acquaintances than parents. He never discussed feelings, interests, wants, or desires with them. He has one brother with whom he does not feel close. He did not often see his brother.

Delbert claimed good relationships with his peers and "hung around with about ten friends." He did not date often, but dated more while he was on heroin.

Psychological Data

Delbert was referred by the adolescent clinic to the psychologist to determine the dynamics of problem areas. The psychologist (examiner) found him a soft spoken, "well kept," blond, young man, who was dressed in casual clothes. He was cooperative throughout both interview and testing. The examiner got the impression that Delbert was trying to con him. He kept repeating "how great it was to be off heroin, how great it was to be off Methadone, and how great it was to be alive." His degree of exuberance was somewhat unreal. He was either trying to convince the examiner, himself, or both.

Delbert admitted difficulty in sleeping. He had recently taken an overdose of Nembutal. He reported that he had been on heroin for approximately one and one-half years, he had started the Methadone program, and was now off drugs. He stated that he no longer had a desire for heroin.

The following evaluative procedures were used with Delbert:

Rorschach Technique
Human Figure Drawings
Sentence Completion Test
Informal Projectives
MMPI
Bender-*Gestalt* Reproductions

Judging from word usage Delbert gives the impression of above average intellectual ability. However, his thinking was rigid and stereotyped. His thinking was also grandiose and unrealistic. Apparently he was building himself up for a let-down in his freedom from heroin use. His ambition is far from reality based.

He sees himself as an ineffective person who must resort to mischievous and manipulative means to achieve his ends. He was observed to be immature, anxious, and moderately depressed young man. He expected things to happen for him rather than making opportunities for himself. He felt his needs of dependency, affection and attention to be unmet. He tried to give the appearance of self-confidence, when actually he lacked it. When faced with problems, however, he still tended to act impulsively. He was over-sensitive and too excitable.

Delbert experienced his mother as a domineering, powerful, controlling person. He felt that she did not understand him at all. His father was seen as a very frightening person. He did state that his relationship with his father was better than in the past.

Delbert's social relationships were superficial. His emotional responsiveness was shallow. He could not enter into a close, meaningful, interpersonal relationship. He projected his own manipulative tendencies on to others. This perception further induced him to withdraw from a close interpersonal relationship. To a stranger he would appear to be guarded and negativistic. His primary defenses were intellectualization, fantasy (daydreams), and massive denial.

In summary, Delbert was an adolescent with above average intelligence, who presented himself as euphoric and highly self-confident. He tried too hard to project this appearance though, with the result that it did not ring true. Actually, he was severely anxious, moderately depressed, and dependent, with a reaction to life that was totally passive. Under stress he reacted without thinking through his actions and their probable results. Any actions that were instigated by him were geared to meet unmet needs of dependence, affection and attention.

It was recommended that Delbert receive supportive counseling with an emphasis on reality. Structuring was very important to Delbert. Due to his over-reaction to stress, close tabs should be kept on him by his counselor. If his bubble should burst, he might return to heroin. He needs constant emotional support. It was recommended that he be evaluated for possible anti-depressant medication. Any counselor should beware of being duped by apparent self-confidence and euphoria.

Medical Evaluation

Delbert answered the medical examiner's question: "What is it you want us to try to do?" with: "Help me to stop using heroin."

He also stated that he wanted off heroin because it was affecting his whole life. He said that he wanted to work, was interested in vocational rehabilitation, completing education in night school, then college. He wanted Methadone treatment.

He had been "shooting" daily for eight months when he came to the medical examiner. He had also experimented with speed and acid.

Delbert had the usual childhood diseases and immunizations. He was currently recovering from chronic hepatitis, probably serum in origin.

The physical examination: weight was 130 lbs., height 70″; acne; hair, dry; dental, fair; posture, normal; audiometer test, passed. His heart, lungs, muscle tonality, etc. were normal. The diagnosis was: heroin addiction, serum hepatitis.

Delbert was put on Methadone treatment and referred to vocational rehabilitation.

Vocational Evaluation

Delbert's vocational history can be briefly stated. His only working experience was in a car wash. He expressed interest in art and law. He expected to finish high school at night then go to college, maybe to study law.

Educational History

Up until the time Delbert dropped out of school, in the eleventh grade, he was doing well. His achievement in most subjects were average to high. On the Differential Aptitude Test he performed extremely well: verbal 93-98 percentile band, quantitative 50-77 percentile band, total 84-90 percentile band. On the Kuhlman-Anderson I.Q. he tested on different occasions 104 and 107. On the Lorge-Thorndike Intelligence Test he tested: verbal I.Q. 131, non-verbal 109, total 120.

Narrative

The client is currently continuing on Methadone treatment. He is also doing well at an adult accelerated learning center. It is expected that he will get a high school equivalent, then be admitted to a local college. He intends to start off in college with general studies, then pre-law.

Because he is severely anxious, moderately depressed, and a dependent individual, supportive counseling is indicated on a long-term basis. Due to a possible over-reaction to stress close tabs must be kept on him, especially during life style choice points and transition periods.

Case Study 23

E. D. W.

White – Male – 21
Single
High School Graduate
Transient situational adjustment reaction to adolescence
Character disorder (inadequate personality with psycho-sexual confusion)
Inability to adjust socially and vocationally characterized by drug abuse

Referral Source

Ernie was referred by the adolescent clinic of a local hospital. His disability was described as "Behavior Disorder – unable to get along with others." Ernie was a 21 year old white male. He was unable to handle stress. Associated with this were extreme dependency needs. Probably because of dependency needs, he sometimes turned to drugs.

Social Evaluation

The client is the product of a prestigious family with high expectations of its members. The father is an attorney; the mother is a secretary to a prominent state official. Ernie has one older sister, three younger sisters and two younger brothers. The mother and father had recently divorced. The client seemed torn between them and this contributed to his identity crisis. Ernie's relation to his family was very much a part of his adjustment problem. He seemed to have a fear of not meeting the parent's expectations. The situation had been complicated by the court's decision to release Ernie to the custody of his father on a 20 year suspended sentence for the sale of heroin. Ernie sees his father as inadequate and a failure. He does not see him as a masculine figure. Ernie's interpersonal relationships were ones of complete dependency.

Psychological Evaluation

Ernie was described as a "tall, slim, good looking adolescent with long hair and the beginnings of a moustache and a beard." Although there existed a degree of anxiety about the tests, he was cooperative. He claimed there were many "geniuses" in his family, and that he was afraid to find out that he was not as intelligent as them.

The WAIS was used with Ernie. The objective results were: Verbal IQ, 136; Performance IQ, 114; Full Scale IQ, 128. He was in the superior range in intelligence. His highest score was in immediate rote memory and concentration. In the performance area his highest score was in knowledge of the social amenities and his lowest score was in putting together familiar objects from their component parts. Obviously his intellectual strengths were in the verbal area. His manual dexterity was average to below average.

The evaluation above was for a referral by the rehabilitation counselor concerned for the purpose of determining intellectual functioning in order that the client could continue in college. An earlier evaluation was given to investigate ego strength and personality dynamics. On the earlier evaluation the following procedures were used:

Bender-Visual Motor *Gestalt* Test
House-Tree-Person-Person
Rorschach Technique
Thematic Apperception Test
Minnesota Multiphasic Personality Inventory

Ernie appeared composed but this could have been due to a prior dosage of Valium - 5 mg. and Methadone 10 mg. He is an "exceptionally bright," well read young man. He discussed drugs, family problems and past experiences logically and articulately. He described a recent hospitalization as a result of an acute aggressive outburst after an argument with girl friend and another argument with his mother over the family car. He said his father and mother were divorced and his father had remarried. Ernie had recently been released to his father by the court on a 20 year suspended sentence for the sale of heroin.

Ernie seems to be a depressed and anxious young man, with anxiety moderated by medication.

The test results showed Ernie anxious "to the point of near panic." A psychotic reaction was evident over a severe identity crisis. By obsessive-compulsive defenses he was attempting to make some order out of his chaos and confusion, but his defenses were fragmenting. With emotion his thinking became loose and autistic; he would grab hold of paranoid grandiosity and religiosity. His defenses were only minimally successful.

The most salient feature about Ernie was his identity crisis. He did not know what to be, male or female, child or adult. He did not seem to be able to accept himself, the good or bad, as elements of a personality. He was striving to meet his family's expectations of social excellence and achievement. He apparently had been so well "socialized" by his parents that his own conscience was castigating him. He felt guilty about not being the paragon of excellence his family expected. He also felt guilty about not filling the roles at home of oldest son, surrogate husband, and substitute father assigned him. It was not a surprise to the evaluator, to say the least, that Ernie was confused about sex role, goals, and general identity. The recent decision by the court, mentioned earlier, probably compounded the schism begun by the parent's divorce. It was suggested by the evaluator that the court decision may have been the precipitator of psychotic behavior recently apparent. A symbiotic dependence upon his mother complicated all else.

Ernie was anxious and depressed. He felt that he was losing his grip on reality and was contemplating suicide. He was afraid of not succeeding financially, emotionally, or socially. Ernie wondered if he could surmount his drug problem. The evaluator suggested that Ernie needed an environment where he would not be "the instrument of his mother's and father's needs." He needed an environment where he could succeed and fail without rejection. Given his abilities, Ernie could work through his problems in the right environment. A strong relationship with a male therapist was suggested by the evaluator.

Medical Evaluation

Ernie had once been in an automobile accident resulting in hospitalization for dislocation of left hemipelvis, separation of the symphysis pubis, lacerations and abrasions. He was fifteen at the time. When he was nineteen years old he was admitted to the hospital for gastroenteritis. This turned out to be withdrawal symptoms from heroin addiction. He was put on methadone treatments.

Other pertinent facts in past history: mumps, measles, varicella, and a motorcycle accident when 18 resulting in right leg fracture.

Diagnosis at time of hospitalization: (1) Gastroenteritis, (2) Adjustment reaction to adolescence with drug abuse and (3) Dermatitis of the right axilla.

Vocational Evaluation

Ernie has had a hodgepodge vocational history. He had worked as a counselor-patient at the adolescent clinic. The staff thought him a valuable asset to their program. He also worked as a rehabilitation counselor aide while associated with vocational rehabilitation. Prior to that he had been associated with general labor, remodeling, insulation, and hotels.

Educational Evaluation

Ernie was an underachiever in high school, being a weak B student. On the Differential Aptitude Tests he scored at the 99th percentile in verbal reasoning and abstract reasoning. He was in the highest percentiles in all else, except mechanical and clerical where he was below average.

After high school Ernie started in college. He withdrew during the first quarter. Later, he entered another college. He received all F's the first quarter attempted. He withdrew the second. Ernie made another attempt at college success while under the auspices of vocational rehabilitation. He received an incomplete, an F, and a B in the three courses attempted.

Ernie has recently disappeared. The rehabilitation counselor working with him does not know his whereabouts.

Rehabilitation Report

The client was declared eligible for services on the basis of "behavior disorder." He was allowed to work with his counselor as a counselor-aide prior to this entrance to college. His attempt at college was a failure. Vocational rehabilitation provided the services of methadone treatments, college tuition, board, room, books, and laundry service.

It is obvious that Ernie has severe problems in identity and dependency needs. His counselor feels, that if he is found, the best placement for him would be with a local drug clinic where drug addicts work with drug addicts. If Ernie could ever work through his problems to the point where he could start sincerely on a constructive course, he would be a valuable asset to the drug clinic, and the clinic a valuable resource for him.

Case Study 24

H. A. W.

White – Male – 23
Single
Completed 11th grade
Toxic psychosis, alcohol and drug addiction

Referral

On July 8, 1972, Mr. W. was court committed to the VA Hospital in Atlanta as a transfer from State Hospital.

Diagnosis

Mr. W. was admitted to State Hospital on July 7, 1972 because he had had a violent temper tantrum in his home. He thought that this outburst was due to alcohol and drug addiction. He admitted that on February 9, 1972 he had been sent to the Naval Hospital because of a similar outburst, which he also thought was caused by drugs. Mr. W. admitted to glue sniffing and smoking marijuana in the past. During the intake staffing, the examining psychiatrist diagnosed Mr. W. as having toxic psychosis and a possible schizophrenic reaction.

Evaluation

On July 9, 1972, Mr. W. was interviewed concerning his social history. The history of his family showed that his father had been an alcoholic, and that his mother had a nervous breakdown on several occasions. Mr. W. completed the 11th grade in school then dropped out in order to join the service. While in the service, he passed all his GED tests, except one section. He is a Vietnam veteran and since his discharge a year ago has been employed as an iron worker. He has been on drugs since his return from Vietnam and at the present time is very anxious to "kick" his habit.

This same day Mr. W. was evaluated in the Department of Physical Medicine & Rehabilitation. He showed good contact with reality and no apparent signs of psychosis. He was then assigned to manual arts therapy in the print shop and also to corrective therapy.

Because of his violent outbursts prior to his hospital admittance, he was then evaluated by the EEG Clinic. The electroencephalographer found that his EEG was within normal limits, and that there were no localizing signs nor signs of seizure discharges present.

On July 29, 1972, Mr. W. went to the Psychology Service in order to obtain vocational counseling and testing. A battery of vocational tests was administered. The results showed that he had vocational interests in the mechanical area (Lee Thorpe Occupational Interest Inventory and the Minnesota Vocational Interest Inventory).

During Mr. W.'s stay in the hospital, he has gotten along well and has been cooperative and sincere in his attitude. He has, however, shown some restlessness and nervousness. He seemed very anxious to avoid any situations in the future which might precipitate his wanting to return to alcohol and drugs as measures of relief from such situations. He showed an eagerness to leave the hospital and to resume working at this former occupation of auto mechanic.

Provision & Arrangement of Service

On August 15, 1972, Mr. W. completed and passed the last section of his GED test. This achievement gained him the status of high school graduate. He also went to the Counseling Psychology Service in order to inquire about referral for job placement. The Office of DVR was contacted in order to arrange for follow-up after placement so that his vocational development and educational training interests could be discussed at any time he wished.

Placement

The Counseling Psychology Service recontacted Mr. W's former employer. The employer, Mr. Jacks, who is a foreman, expressed a willingness to re-employ Mr. W. upon his discharge. He said that

Mr. W. had performed well when there before and that he had a good mechanical aptitude. He believed that Mr. W. was eligible for a higher level job than he had previously held especially since he obtained the high school equivalency diploma. He, however, wanted to rehire him on a 30 day trial period.

On August 16, 1972, Mr. W. was discharged from the hospital and returned to his former place of employment on the following day.

Follow-Up

After completing a 30 day trial period on the job as an auto mechanic, he began on the job training (OJT) in the same plant as an assistant foreman. At the DVR Office during the following week, he and his family discussed his vocational development with a rehabilitation counselor.

Case Study 25

P. A. R.

White – Female – 19 – Single
High School Graduate
Behavior disability. Inability to adjust due to drug abuse.

Referral Source

Miss R. was referred to the vocational rehabilitation counselor by the city's medical drug treatment center following extensive treatment and counseling about her drug addiction. She was referred because of drug addiction and drug misuse, characterized by inability to adjust and function in society. Her doctors feel she is now ready to benefit from treatment and counseling. She was referred for counseling and possible college training.

In the opinion of clinic doctors, rehabilitation counseling is the best solution to her drug abuse problem.

Social History

Miss R. is a nineteen year old attractive, white female. She comes from a home environment where constant arguing among all members of the family took place. Her parents were constantly fighting, and Miss R. felt this was due to her father's "jealousy" of her mother. Her father is forty-eight years old and works as a real estate appraiser. Her mother is forty-four years old and works as a clerk in a local department store. Miss R. has two younger brothers age twelve and age nine, who have recently begun to resent her.

Miss R. admits using drugs for about two years. She started by smoking grass and then went to LSD and then on to heroin. Her drug activities increased when she met her current boy friend. Miss R. related to the counselor that she had been promiscuous for some time. She mentioned briefly about leaving home "after getting fed up with her family and their old fashioned attitudes." Miss R. said she "digs" drugs and plans to continue using grass despite what has happened to her with heroin.

According to Miss R's parents, she had many friends both boys and girls, until she met and started dating her present boy friend. Once she started "hanging around him," all her friends deserted her. Miss R. ran away with her boy friend one spring for two weeks. Her parents made no attempt to contact her personally but sent a note to her by a cousin saying she could come home if she wished. Both of her parents feel that she has had a complete change in personality since she met this boy. They feel she has become "impossible" and uncommunicable.

One specific event which caused her mother much concern occurred when Mrs. R. drove her daughter to school. That morning, Miss R. cussed her mother all the way to school for no apparent reason. Both parents feel that Miss R. has never been close to them.

She began dating in late adolescence because no one would ask her out since she looked so young. In senior high school she dated very much. She argued a great deal with her parents about later hours for dates. To them she also seemed to be jealous of her brothers. Miss R. always complained that they had more than she did. Her parents feel she always abused her privileges, no matter how lenient they were or how much they trusted her.

Miss R. was recently "busted" for heroin possession. Her case went to court and she was placed on probation. She now lives at home and is working for a church organization. This work consists of helping with underprivileged children in a disadvantaged area. Her parents feel that because of this work Miss R. was doing well. She was dating and apparently back into the "main stream" with adolescent peers.

Six months later, Miss R. came to the adolescent clinic stating that she had been using large quantities of heroin in a communal type setting. She had used non-sterile needles and syringes for injection of heroin. She requested to be placed on Methadone in order to withdraw from heroin.

General Medical History

Previous history of communicable disease reveals Miss R. has contracted the usual childhood diseases. At the age of seven, she was hospitalized for eight months for an allergic reaction to poison ivy.

She has been addicted to heroin for two years. She started with grass and progressed to LSD. She then met a boy who introduced her to "smack" (heroin). She was given counseling and placed on the withdrawal drug methadone. Miss R. is no longer involved with drugs.

Two weeks before entering the drug clinic, Miss R. used a needle from a user who had a known case of hepatitus. She was given gamma globin injections (10ccs). Later examinations of this client reveals she had been feeling fine. She had no evidence of hepatitus, no tenderness in the right upper quadrant, and no evidence of ieterus of the sclera.

Physical Examination

GENERAL APPEARANCE	thin/withdrawn, adult female
HEIGHT without shoes	63¼″
WEIGHT	96 (15# underweight)
VISION	without glasses – normal
	with glasses – normal
	1.50 test – normal
PHROIAE	Distant – normal
	Hor. – normal
	Vert. – normal
NEAR HORIZONTAL	normal
COLOR VISION	normal
SKIN	Color – pale
	Pigmentation – normal
	Dry
	Eruptions – acne – no
	leterus – no
	Pallor – no
	Palms – moist
	Vaccination Scar – yes
	Other scars – antinbital from 2″ needle/both arms
HAIR	dry
EARS	Hearing – normal
	Canals – normal
	Drums – normal

EYES	Pupils – Equal – normal
	React to light – normal
	Accommodation – normal
	Extraocular Movements – normal
	Conjunctivae – normal
	Exophthalmus – normal
	Fundi – normal
NOSE	Obstruction – none
	Sinus Tenderness – none
MOUTH AND THROAT	Oral Hygiene – good
	Gums – good
	Caries – none
	Tonsils – removed
	Thyroid – normal
LYMPH GLANDS	normal
THORAX	Deformity – none
LUNGS	clear
B. P.	(recumbant) 100/60
HEART	normal
ABDOMEN	normal
GENITALIA	Stage of Development – Stage V – menstruating
	Hernia – no
	Pilondial Sinus – no
NEUROLOGICAL	Gait – normal
	Strength – good
	Coordination – good
	Balance – good
	Reflexes – good
EXTREMITIES	Paralysis, atrophy – normal
	Feet – normal
POSTURE	Neck – normal
	shoulders – normal
	Spine – (curvature) normal
	tenderness – none
HABITS	Nail Biting – no
	Tic – no
	Speech – good

The pertinent physical findings were limited to needle marks in both anticubital fossea that appeared to be healing without complications. The only other physical findings noteworthy is mild ephlgastric discomfort and right upper quadrant discomfort with deep palpitations of those areas.

Laboratory studies included: 1) a growth curve of weight and height by age for girls, which indicated she was approximate for her height. 2) Blood count serology, calcium, inorganic, phorpherous, glucose, BUN, uric acid, cholesteral, total protein, albumin, total bilirubin, alkaline phosphatase, LDH and SGOT. All these laboratory studies were within normal limits as reported by the clinical laboratory at the City Hospital.

Educational History

Miss R. was graduated from high school with an interest in business. At the beginning her high school career, she maintained grades of A's and B's. Gradually her grades dropped to C's, D's, and F's. School had always been somewhat of a problem for her. She had difficulty in getting along with teachers. Because of this Miss R. was often truant during her three high school years and she was expelled from school many times.

Psychological Data

She is a bright young woman who has rather long term emotional problems which have been generally unrecognized by her parents. These problems finally erupted when she was arrested for heroin possession. She has skipped school, been promiscuous, used drugs, and lied to her parents about most of her activities for some time. It is felt that she is not physiologically addicted but may be psychologically dependent on stimulants.

Miss R. appears to be completely "lost." She has a far away bewildered look in her eyes, but answers questions without difficulty.

Diagnosis: Behavior disorder, adjustment reaction characterized by drug abuse.

Vocational History

Miss R's principal employment has been as a telephone operator on afternoons after school. This job was in relation with her business courses. She stated that she did not particularly like her job but did enjoy making the money. During the summers she was unemployed and at the time of referral to rehabilitation she had no employment.

Her primary interests include progressive rhythm and blues, "nature," and bike riding. She had mentioned a desire to go to college and major in business.

Eligibility

Miss R's disability has been diagnosed as drug addiction characterized by an inability to adjust socially. She had been seen by the City Clinic for drug abuse and is no longer involved with drugs. She has been to court for drug possession but was not committed to an institution. She was placed on probation. The limitation from this disability constitutes a substantial handicap to employment. She has been trying to find steady employment but is having difficulty due to her previous record with drugs. Miss R. has had several part time jobs but has been unable to hold any of these jobs for any length of time. There is reasonable expectation that VR services will render her fit for gainful employment.

Plan

Vocational Objective : Teacher

It was felt by all members of the helping team that Miss R. has the ability and now the stability to continue her education. She is interested in becoming a teacher. She has been accepted by City University as a special student this semester, taking nine hours and will become enrolled as a full time student in February.

Services Provided

VR will furnish tuition, fees and books. Upon completion of college, training, placement and follow-up will be rendered.

Tuition and Fees	$225.00
Books	50.00
Total Cost Rendered	$277.00

Summary

Miss R. as a special student at City University took the following courses:

Introduction to Philosophy
Cultural Anthropology
English Literature I

She received withdrawals for all courses. Her withdrawal from school was due to a physical problem related to her drug abuse. She developed hepatitus which required her to be away from school for a long period of time.

The doctor and school administrator feel she should return to school next semester. She is showing much progress socially and emotionally.

While Miss R. was at home recovering from hepatitus, emotional problems developed which precipitated her return to drug usage. She is currently under treatment and progressing well. The rehabilitation counselor and her treatment physician feel that she should move out of the home where her emotional problems continue to develop. When Miss R. has progressed sufficiently, she will proceed toward her vocational objective.

Case Study 26

J. W. W.

White – Male – 17
Single
Passive-Aggressive Personality disturbance with depression; Anti-social Personality Features. Drug abuse characterized by an inability to adjust vocationally and socially

Referral Source

James was referred to the Department of Vocational Rehabilitation by Dr. Smith of the City Hospital Adolescent Clinic. The vocational rehabilitation counselor met with Dr. Smith, who informed him that James' parents brought him to the clinic because of his poor school records, poor attendance and attitudes, non-conformity with normal dress standards, lack of self discipline and dependability. Several attempts were made by the parents to enter James in private school before bringing him to the clinic. James has no previous work experience.

Social Data

James is a 17 year old, long haired-bearded, young man. He is a tall, good looking boy who looks older and more physically mature than his seventeen years. James comes from a family which is unstable and cold. He has been brought up in an environment where alcoholism and castigation are very much a part of the family atmosphere.

James has no interests and no plans for the future. He has not thought about college because he does not think he could make it. He likes sports, but only as a spectator. Mostly, he just "messes around" with his friends. The father is 46 years old and is described as nice looking, overindulging in alcohol intake, making weak efforts to assert himself and to be the strong one in the family. He is perceived by others as weak and not wanting to take on responsibility. He tries to control his violence and does not believe in physical punishment. He was the ninth of nine children and the only boy. He claims that he is "incapable of love" and only feels close to people if he drinks. He went into the military career because his wife disliked that career. The family has moved around a lot. He admitted the marriage to be a failure. He came from a broken home, paternal grandparents separated when he was 13 years old and he left home for good at age 15. He had three years of college; is a retired Lt. Colonel in the Army and has been working for 5 years as assistant Personnel Officer at the Highway Department. He described himself as "a cold, hearted SOB." It is too late to change. He also stated that there is no hope for his marriage. His mother is living in the home and he claims she interferes with the rearing of the children.

The mother is 47 years old, very attractive, the stronger one of the family and she describes herself as "having a big mouth." She feels the child needs limits; she is quick tempered and the marriage is perceived by her as ungratifying. They have split several times and reunited again. She admitted being somewhat rejecting of the child since the very beginning. She had a "nervous breakdown" just before the child was conceived. The mother had a very unhappy childhood; her father was gassed in World War I and was hospitalized when she was a year old. He was in a Virginia hospital for some time and died later in 1936. She never had close contact with the maternal grandfather but she wants to make a hero out of him. She finished high school and wants to work. She considers her marriage a failure; she is status oriented. Apparently there has been a lot of verbal abuse in the family between the parents and between parents and the children. She feels that at the present moment she is at the verge of a nervous breakdown if the family does not get help. She feels that her husband is sick and considers money the most important thing. They are on the verge of bankruptcy.

There were four children in this family; Joey, 21, is described as a "con artist," senior at college in engineering; Pete, 19, is a freshman at City University, a loner, diligent, questionable epileptic; George, 17, "has strong likes and dislikes." James is the youngest of the children. He is in City High School in the 10th grade but is apparently taking 9th and 10th grade subjects. During the interview with the counselor, he denied problems with the law. He admitted running away to Florida, in May 1969; stayed there about a week with a group of boys. While in Florida one of the boys called his parents. James' parents left the decision up to him as to whether or not to come home. He admitted staying out late with friends and at times not returning home. He claims he is the baby in the family. He has used marijuana once but "didn't feel that much." He claims he did not obtain a kick. James admittedly informed this counselor that he has used heroin for a period of time. However, he enjoys the euphoria he gets from injecting seconal and other barbiturates. He uses barbiturates intravenously daily.

Medical Data

James stated that he had been in good general health. He has used marijuana, heroin and barbiturates intravenously but is not yet physically addicted. He experienced the normal childhood diseases and has been in good health since birth.

GENERAL MEDICAL EXAMINATION

HEIGHT	5′11″
WEIGHT	169 lbs.
VISION	20/20
COLOR VISION	normal
SKIN	Color – Caucasian
	Eruptions – scars
	Pallor – normal
	Dry – dry
	Iceterus – normal
	Vaccination scars – yes
HAIR	dry
EARS	normal
EYES	normal
NOSE	normal
MOUTH AND THROAT	normal
THORAX	normal
LUNGS	normal
BLOOD PRESSURE	138/78
HEART	normal

ABDOMEN	normal
GENITALIA	normal – stage V
NEUROLOGICAL	normal
FEET	normal
POSTURE	good
HABITS	Nail Biting – positive
PERSONALITY TRAITS	Tense – Quite withdrawn

Educational Data

James has had severe problems in adjusting to the academic climate in the public educational system. He was doing adequate work in school until he reached the sixth grade. He began exhibiting antisocial behavior in the classroom and his grades began to fall. His behavior became more intense as he moved from one grade to the next. A truancy record began and James had several run-ins with the school officials. His grades in high school were C's, D's, and F's.

Psychological Data

James was administered a battery of tests consisting of the Weschsler Intelligence Scale, Wide Range Achievement Test, Bender Visual Motor *Gestalt* Test and the Rorschach Test.

James achieved a V-IQ of 106, a P-IQ of 100 and a Full Scale of 104 on the WISC, which placed him in the average range of intellectual function. He showed little impairment of his basic ability which may fall within the Bright Normal range. There were no test signs of strong anxiety or visual-motor rigidity to create his very mildly depressed performance, only an erratic involvement without much motivation or attention to details. His pattern of performance was fairly consistent, with no focal high or low points. He was equally proficient with both verbal and visual motor tasks.

Despite his poor grades, James has been absorbing and retaining basic academic skills. His Wide Range Achievement Test (WRAT) reading score was 12.6; his word approach was syllabic and phonetic and he showed no hesitation at unfamiliar words. His arithmetic score is lower, 9.5 but roughly consistent with placement. Three of his failures were on the simplest computations which required at the most 5th grade achievement. Again, no overt anxiety created this loss, but a hasty uninvolved approach.

His Bender-*Gestalt* shows no signs of central nervous system involvement, but does indicate a youthful egocentricity, with failures to plan ahead and anticipate. James appears to be unable to tolerate much stress and under its impact, responds with some impulsivity but not a devastating loss of control.

With adolescent immaturity, he tends to act on impulse, seeking self-gratification, but is not an aggressive, hostile boy and is not lacking in empathy and identification with others. His emotional responses are somewhat under-controlled, but are not volatile. He can achieve an impersonal matter-of-fact approach.

There are no serious distractions of reality or bizarre ideation, although James does over-generalize and jump to hasty conclusions. While he is capable of better logic and integration, he seems to feel no necessity for it and does not apply any intellectual criticism or analysis – he simply responds.

He shows some negativism and a need to assert himself in a stubborn fashion to work himself free from a relationship in which he sees himself as dependent and subordinate. Typically he acts with self-assuredness, failing to question his own motives or behavior. James appears to be responding to an overcontrolling mother and is experiencing the mild rebellion and independence seeking of adolescence, but without any indication of intense hostility or inter-personal withdrawal.

Abstract from Psychiatric Report

James' developmental history is non-contributing except for the fact that he was an unwanted child, his mother tried to obtain an abortion but she could not get one. She denied taking any steps to abort herself. James is a 17 year old boy who appears more mature and older physically than his given age. He had a long standing history of acting out. Apparently he is committed to act out antisocially and has been in constant trouble with the law since the age of 10. He comes from a very pathological family; father is an alcoholic, weak, unable to relate to members of the family and has serious personality problems. The mother appears to be domineering, inconsistent and rejecting of this child since conception. She has apparently tried to keep the child from trouble, but her efforts have been ineffectual. James has witnessed tremendous amounts of disrespect between his parents and does not find them as models for identification. He has felt unstable, insecure, and very threatened at home. This is a severely characterologically damaged child with severe pathology and with a great deal of conflicts which he is acting out antisocially. He has no internalized external controls. James' prognosis is very poor. He wants to be away from home and feels he cannot tolerate the situation much longer.

Diagnosis

1. Passive aggressive personality disturbance with depression. Antisocial personality features.
2. Drug abuse characterized by an inability to adjust vocationally and socially.

James left home and enlisted in the Army. He is now serving with NATO forces in Europe.

Case Study 27

G. A. L

White – Male – 24 – Single
Third Year College
Schizophrenic catatonic with drug addiction (multiple addiction)
Subsequent diagnosis:
Schizophrenic, paranoid with drug addiction (multiple addiction)

Referral Source

Glen was twenty-four years old at the time of referral. He is Caucasian. Glen was in the Navy, stationed in Naples, Italy, when one morning he refused to get out of bed. He was then referred to the U. S. Naval Hospital, Naples. At the hospital he was uncommunicative, inappropriate in affect, and austic. From Naples Glen was sent to U. S. Naval Hospital Bethesda, Maryland. At Bethesda, Glen was diagnosed as having schizophrenic reaction, catatonic type (later diagnosis – paranoid), and as a drug addict (multiple addiction). Finally, Glen was referred to a Veterans Administration Hospital.

Social Evaluation

Glen went to college for three and one-half years prior to joining the Navy. He got "wrapped up" in drug culture while in college. He took heroin and marijuana himself; he also "pushed" drugs.

Glen has a younger brother and a younger sister, 15 and 22 respectively. The sister married her stepbrother. The mother has remarried since his father's death six years ago.

He was never really close to his natural father nor his mother. When he needed someone to talk to he would go to the maternal grandmother who died three years ago. Glen feels that his mother and stepfather do not want him around. Since his grandmother is dead, he feels that he has no one.

Glen worked for a year in Australia, while in the company of his parents, as a construction worker. He met a girl there and fell in love. They planned to get married. While he was away she met another fellow and married him. Glen met her again in Naples. She was pregnant and getting a divorce. Glen made love to her while she was in Naples. They planned to marry after the divorce. This new meeting with her seems to have precipitated the schizo-catatonic reaction and return to drugs. She returned to London, England. He was transferred from the Naval Hospital in Naples to the Naval Hospital in Atlanta, Georgia. While there Glen received a "Dear John" from the girl saying she had returned to her husband in London. Glen left the hospital and flew to London but was not allowed to leave the airport because he did not have the proper papers. He called his girl from the airport, but she refused to meet him. He returned to the hospital.

Psychological Evaluation

Glen was referred to U. S. Naval Hospital, Naples for reasons indicated earlier. He related the story about his girl: about arranging to meet her in Naples, her pregnancy, divorce, etc. He also expressed hostile feelings about her pregnancy, telling about how at one meeting he pounded her abdomen with his head, hoping for an abortion. She visited him while he was in the hospital. After the meeting he was euphoric for a while.

A mental examination depicted Glen as a bearded young man who stared constantly at the floor. He occasionally, with a smile, cautiously touched the examiner's hand. Sometimes he "aped" the movements of the examiner. Affect was obtunded. Glen was morose. Once he made a ceremonial march to the couch and curled up fetus-like. The impression of the examiner was that Glen was grossly psychotic with a schizophrenic reaction, catatonic type.

After Glen's trip to London to see his "girl friend" had failed he was euphoric for a while. Later he was caught "mainlining" heroin in the hospital. He stated that drugs were a "substitute for his girl friend." It was then felt that Glen could no longer be managed in an open ward. So, it was recommended that he be transferred for further treatment.

At the Veterans Administration Hospital, Glen's past history with drugs in college was discovered. He had gotten to the point in college so that the drug scene was all that mattered to him. He dropped out of college in his third year. He then joined the service.

At this hospital also Glen related the story about his girl. He also talked of forming a commune with four women and three men where there would be sexual freedom. He thought he could prove in the commune that he was not running away from society in that six other people would be living in the commune.

In later interviews Glen still had grandiose ideas "about starting a new society in the form of a commune." He also showed ambivalence by saying that he could not condone killing animals but felt morally right about killing a fetus. Glen also exhibited paranoid delusions. He feared that doctors, x-ray machines, and others were attempting to damage his internal organs.

In testing, Glen was evasive and uncooperative. His scores on the WAIS were: Verbal IQ 105, Performance 108, and Full Scale 107. He had had over two years of college and possible deterioration was indicated.

Medical Evaluation

Glen, 5′9″, weight 153, had only the normal childhood diseases: measles, mumps, etc. His physical functioning at present is normal.

Vocational History

Glen worked as a construction worker in Australia for a year. He has been an aviation electronic technician in the Navy.

Educational History

Glen dropped out of college in his third year. He has also finished a computer school but never worked with computers. He has had training in the service in electronics. He expresses a desire to finish his schooling.

Narrative

Glen is still considered a schizo-catatonic with paranoid tendencies. He has shown some improvement. He states that he likes the hospital and would like to stay there until discharge. After discharge he hopes to continue college. When he was allowed to go home for Christmas he suffered a setback, returned to drugs and came back to the hospital suffering from toxicity and withdraw symptoms. He states that he wants his mother and stepfather to "want" him. It is hoped that with further treatment, and with time between the traumatic experience with the girl, Glen will successfully adjust to life. His situation at present is at best uncertain.

Chapter 3

LANGUAGE OF THE DRUG ABUSER

THIS section offers a glossary of the language of the drug user. The glossary is in no way complete, but every effort has been made to select those words and terms which may be used most frequently. The reader should remember that the use of these words varies dramatically among geographic regions. A word which is popular in one area may be used very seldom in another.

These words represent the word usage of many addicts throughout the country; however, it is doubtful that any one addict would be familiar with all the included terms.

The argot which addicts use gives a clear description of their way of life. From the terms the reader will be able to discern the compensatory use of drugs by the individual with an inadequate personality and the necessity for many users for escape from reality. Many of the words in the language of the addict are words or modifications used originally by opium smokers, and a number of these words are oriental in origin.

If professionals are to be of help to members of drug culture, they not only must understand the language of the drug abuser but also must have a feeling for the differences in his perceptions of words and his use of language. Work done by the authors (Cull and Hardy, 1973a; Cull and Hardy, 1973b; and Hardy and Cull, 1973) indicate sub-cultural groups use language in decidedly different fashions. Racial differences and differences in physical capacities cause individuals to use and perceive everyday language in an altered fashion. Consequently, professionals who work with drug abusers must understand the jargon of this group. This glossary is only the first step in developing this understanding.

GLOSSARY

A

Abe – A Five-Dollar Bill
Acapulco Gold – A high quality of Marijuana.
Acid – LSD (Lysergic Acid Diethylamide). Hallucinogen.
Acid Dropper – One who uses LSD.
Acid Freak – A Habitual user of LSD, Cube Head.
Acid Head – LSD user.
Action – The selling of narcotics. Anything pertaining to criminal activities.
Alcohol – Booze, Juice.
Amp. – A 1-cc Methedrine Ampule, legitimate.
Amphetamines – Stimulants which are generally Dexedrine, Benzedrine, Methedrine, or Biphetamine. Bambita, Bennies, Bottles, Browns, Cart-wheels, Chicken Powder, Co-pilots, Dexies, Eye openers, Footballs, Greenies, Hearts, Jolly Beans, Jugs, LA Turnabouts, Lid Proppers, Orangies, Peaches, Pep Pills, Roses, Speed, Truck Drivers, Ups, Wake Ups, Whites.
Amys – Amyl Nitrate, Stimulant.
Angel Dust – PCP, an animal tranquilizer.
Artillery – Equipment for injecting drugs.
Away – In jail.
Axe – Musical Instrument.

B

Back up – A condition in which blood backs up into the syringe while injecting a drug into the vein.
Backtrack – To make sure a needle is in proper position when mainlining by withdrawing the plunger of the syringe before actually injecting the drugs.
Bad Trip – Bummer.
Bag – Situation; category.
Bag – An envelope of Heroin (see Nickel Bag and Dime Bag).
Bagman – An individual who sells drugs.
Bambita – Desoxyn or Amphetamine Derivative.
Bambs – Barbiturates.
Band House – Jail.
Bang – Fix, shot; injection of narcotics.
Barbiturates – Sedatives, usually Seconal, Nembutal, Amutal, Luminal, Tuinal. Barbs, Blue Heavens, Double Trouble, Nimbie, Peanuts, Purple

Hearts, Rainbows, Red Devils, Sleeping Pills, Yellow Jackets.

Barbs – Barbiturates.

Bay State – A standard medical hypodermic syringe, usually made of glass with metal reinforcement, using a plunger and screw-type needle.

Bean Trip – Intoxication from ingesting Benzedrine; a Benny Jag.

Beat – To cheat or out bargain.

Bee that stings – A drug habit, especially one coming on; "a monkey on my back."

Belt – The euphoria following an injection of narcotics. A shot, or a quantity of drugs to be injected.

Bennies – Benzedrine.

Benny Jag – Intoxication from ingesting Benzedrine.

Bernice – Cocaine.

Bhang – Marijuana.

Big C – Cocaine.

Big D – LSD.

Big John – The police or any law enforcement officer.

Bindle – A small package of narcotics.

Bit – A prison sentence.

Black and White – A policeman.

Black Beauty – Speed in a black capsule.

Blackjack – Paregoric which has been cooked down to be injected in a concentrated form.

Blank – Bag of non-narcotic powder sold as a regular bag (also Dummy, Turkey).

Blanks – Gelatin capsules supposedly filled with a drug which are actually filled only with milk powder or sugar powder or sugar cubes supposedly saturated with LSD which have only food color.

Blasted – Under the influence of drugs.

Blast Party – Group gathered to smoke Marijuana.

Blotter – A piece of absorbent paper on which LSD has been absorbed.

Blow – To lose something; to smoke Marijuana.

Blow a Pill – To smoke Opium.

Blow a Stick – To smoke a Marijuana cigarette.

Blow Snow – To sniff Cocaine.

Blow Weed – To smoke Marijuana.

Blue Birds – Blues, Barbiturates.

Blue Devil – Amobarbital sodium in solid blue form.

Blue Heavens – Barbiturates.

Blue Mist – A sugar cube colored blue by an LSD preparation.

Blues – Barbiturate.

Blue Velvet – Sodium Amytal, Pyribenzamine.
Bombido – Injectible Amphetamine (Also Jugs, Bottles).
Boost – Steal.
Booster – A professional shoplifter, male or female.
Boot – Pushing and pulling the plunger of a syringe to cause a "rush."
Booze – Alcohol.
Bottles – Injectible Amphetamines.
Boy – Heroin.
Bread – Money.
Brick – A kilogram of Marijuana compressed under pressure to retain the shape of a brick.
Browns – Long acting Amphetamine Sulfate (capsules, many colors mainly brown).
Buffotenine – A drug chemically related to DMT derived from dried glandular secretions of certain toads as well as from the *amanita* fungus.
Bum Beef – False complaint or information which usually is given deliberately to the police.
Bum Kick – Boring, unpleasant.
Bum Rap – An arrest or conviction for a crime the man actually did not commit, as distinguished from denying it.
Bum Steer – See Bum Beef.
Bum Trip or Bummer – A bad trip on LSD.
Bundle – Twenty-five $5 bags of Heroin.
Burned – Rendered useless or vulnerable by recognition; e.g. "A narcotic agent was *burned* and unable to continue surveillance." Also, to receive non-narcotic or highly diluted drugs.
Bust or Busted – Arrested; broke.
Buttons – See Mescaline.
Buy – A narcotic peddler; a purchase of narcotics.

C

Caballo – Heroin.
Cactus – See Peyote.
Cactus Buttons – See Mescaline.
Can – A car; A city Jail.
Candy – Barbiturates.
Cap – A person, especially a young Black, who has to hustle to support his habit. Also, a gelatine capsule or a capsule of drugs.
Cartwheels – Amphetamine Sulphate in round, white, double-scored tablets.
Cat Nap – To get small (and very welcome) snatches of sleep during the

withdrawal period.
Chalk – Methedrine.
Charas – Marijuana.
Charged Up – Under the influence of drugs.
Charley – Cocaine.
Charley Coke – A Cocaine addict (restricted to New York and New England).
Chicago Leprosy – Multiple absesses.
Chicken Out – Cop out.
Chicken Powder – Amphetamine powder.
Chip – Heroin.
Chipping – Taking narcotics occasionally.
Chippy – Nice-looking girl.
Chloral Hydrate – Joy Juice.
Clear up – To withdraw from drugs.
Clout – To steal, especially as a shoplifter.
Coasting – The sensation of euphoria following the use of a drug. Used of all drugs except Cocaine. Serving an easy prison sentence.
Coast-to-Coast – Long-acting Amphetamine Sulphate in round forms found in many colors. Also LA turnabouts, Co-pilots, Browns.
Cocaine – Bernice, Big C, Charley, Coke, Corine, Dust, Flake, Girl, Gold Dust, Happy Dust, Heaven Dust, Her, Ice, Snow, Star Dust, White Nurse.
Codeine – School Boy.
Cohoba – Powdered seeds used as snuff.
Coke – Cocaine.
Coked Up – Under the influence of Cocaine.
Cold Turkey – Sudden withdrawal without any alleviating drugs.
Come Down – The end of a trip; the depressed feeling when the drug effects are fading.
Connection – A drug supplier.
Contact – A person who has a connection or who knows a supplier of drugs.
Cooker – Bottle top or spoon used for dissolving Heroin in water over flame.
Cook-It-Up – To prepare Heroin (or other Opiates) for injection by heating it in a cooking spoon.
Cool – (adj.) In complete control.
Cool – (v) To wait.
Cop a Fix – To obtain a ration of Narcotics.
Co-pilots – Amphetamines. Also Truck Drivers, Bennies.
Cop or connect – To buy or get; to purchase drugs.
Cop-out – To inform; to pull out or chicken out; to confess; to alibi.
Cop to – Admit to stealing.
Corine – Cocaine

Cotton – The small wisp of cotton placed in the cooking spoon and used as a filter when the solution is drawn up into the needle.

Cotton Head – A narcotics abuser who depletes his supply of Narcotics and attempts to secure one more injection by re-cooking the cotton used from previous fixes.

Crackling Shorts – Breaking into cars.

Crank – Methedrine; stimulant.

Crash – An unpleasant ending of a trip.

Crash Pad – Apartment set up specifically for people to sleep in.

Crib – One's home or apartment. A house of prostitution. A hypochondriac with many persistent symptoms.

Croaker – Unscrupulous doctor who sells drugs or prescriptions to illicit drug users.

Crutch – Device used for holding shortened butt of Marijuana cigarette. See Roach Clip.

Crystal – Methedaine. See Speed.

Cube – LSD on sugar cubes.

Cubehead – See Acid Freak.

Cut – The dilution of a narcotic with substances like lactose (milk sugar) or quinine, strychnine, etc., in order to increase the profit of the drug trafficker.

Cut Out – To leave a certain place.

D

"D" – LSD.

Daisy – A male homosexual. Also Sissy, Queen, Sex Punk.

Dead – No action.

Deal – Sell narcotics to addicts.

Dealer – Anyone who buys or sells stolen goods. A peddler.

Dealing – Keeping on with whatever one is doing; selling dope.

Deck – Several bags of drugs.

Desoxyn – Amphetamine derivative.

DET – A chemically developed hallucinogenic drug; it has not been found occurring in nature.

Deuce – Two-dollar package of Heroin.

Dexies – Dexedrine, stimulant.

Dig – To understand; to follow

Dime Bag – A $10 purchase of Narcotics.

Dirty – Possessing drugs, liable to arrest.

DMT – A hallucinogen found in the seeds of certain plants native to parts of South America and the West Indies. The powdered seeds have been used for centuries as a snuff 'Cohoba."

Dollies – Dolophine; synthetic Heroin.

Dolly – Methadone.

Dolophine – Dollies, synthetic Heroin.

DOM or STP – (4-Methyl-2, 5-Dimethoxyamphetamine) An hallucinogenic drug produced in the laboratory which induces euphoria and other hallucinogenic effects.

Doo Jee – Heroin.

Dope – Narcotics. Information. To drug. This term, like dope fiend, tends to be taboo among addicts, though they use both perjuratively.

Dope Hop – A prison term for drug addicts, mostly used by guards, turn-keys, and police.

Double Trouble – Amobarbital Sodium combined with Seconbarbital Sodium in red and blue capsules.

Down – Basic; depressed.

Downer Freak – A habitual user of "Downers."

Downers – Sedatives, Alcohol, Tranquilizers and Narcotics.

Dragged – A post Marijuana state of anxiety.

Drop – Swallow a drug.

Dropped – Taken orally.

Drug – To annoy.

Dry – Without drugs.

Dummy – A bag of non-narcotic powder sold as a regular bag. Also Blank, Turkey.

Dust – Cocaine.

Dynamite – Something extra special or good.

E

Echos – See Flashback.

Eighth – Eighth of an ounce of Heroin.

Electric – Overpowering, this is a positive statement.

Eye Dropper – Medicine dropper used with hypodermic needle as makeshift syringe. Most addicts actually prefer it to a syringe.

Eye Opener – Amphetamines.

F

Fag – A pimp. Not to be confused with the general slang fag (a homosexual) clipped from faggot.

Fall – To be arrested. To receive a prison sentence. See Bust.

Fat Jay – A Marijuana cigarette approaching the size of a commercial cigarette or larger. They are made large to compensate for weaker types of Marijuana.

Fed – A federal agent, usually a narcotic agent. Also, The Man, Narco.

Finger – Stool pigeon.

Finger Gee – Stool pigeon.

Finger Wave – A rectal examination for contraban narcotics.

Finif or Finski – A $5 bill.

Fink – A stool pigeon; an untrustworthy person. Also wrong, no good, rat.

Five-cent Bag – A $5 Heroin Fix.

Fix – Injection of Narcotics.

Flake – Cocaine.

Flash – A quick jolt of high in abdomen or across chest from Heroin shot.

Flashback – Partial reoccurrence of an LSD trip.

Flea Powder – Grossly inferior Heroin.

Flipped – Becoming psychotic after an overdose of drugs.

Floating – To be high on drugs.

Fly – Sophisticated yet carefree; wise in the ways of the underworld.

Flying – See Floating.

Footballs – Amphetamine sulphate in oval-shaped tablets of various colors. Also Greenies.

Fox – Good-looking girl.

Freak – An individual who is excessive in some area; for example, "Acid Freak" or "Speed Freak."

Freak-out – Bad experience with hallucinogenic drugs.

Fuzz – Policeman or Detective.

G

Gal Head – Narcotics addict.

Ganja – Marijuana.

Garbage – See Flea Powder.

Gee Stick – An Opium Pipe. Obsolescent.

George – Very good.

Get a finger wave – The process of having the rectum searched for drugs.

Gig – Job.

Girl – Cocaine.

Give Wings – To start someone else on Narcotics.

Going Up – Taking drugs, particularly "Uppers."

Gold Dust – Cocaine.
Gold Leaf Special – A Marijuana cigarette which is thought to be very potent.
Goods – Narcotics, especially as they are bought and sold. Used by addicts or dealers in letters, phone calls, or telegrams.
Goof Balls – Barbiturates.
Goofers – See Goof Balls.
Gow – Narcotics in general, especially those used hypodermically.
Grapes – Wine.
Grass – Marijuana.
Greenies – Amphetamine Sulphate (oval shaped tablets).
Green Score – Profit made by passing counterfeit money.
Gun – Hypodermic needle for injecting Heroin.

H

"H" – Heroin.
Hack – A physician.
Hairy – Heroin.
Hang Tough – Take it easy, quiet down, stop.
Hang Up – A problem, generally a personal problem or a psychological problem.
Happy Dust – Cocaine.
Hard Stuff – Narcotics.
Harpoon – The hallow needle used with a joint. Also Spike, Silver Serpent, Pin, Machine, Tom Cat.
Harry – Heroin.
Hashish or Hash – Marijuana.
Hawk – LSD.
Hay – Marijuana.
Head – A user of drugs. Usually a user of LSD.
Hearts – Dextoamphetamine Sulphate in orange-colored heart-shaped tablets. Also Orangies, Dexies, Peaches, Bennies, Roses.
Heat – Police or Detective.
Heaven Dust – Cocaine.
Heavy – Deep or profound.
Heeled – See Dirty.
Hemp – Marijuana.
Henry – Heroin.
Her – Cocaine.
Heroin – Boy, Caballo, Doo Jee, "H," Hairy, Harry, Henry, Horse, Joy Powder, Junk, Scag, Scat, Skit, Smack, Stuff, Tecata, White Lady, White Nurse.

High – Under the influence of drugs.
Hip – Aware.
Hippies – Those who like to associate with jazzmen, many of whom are drug users.
Hit – To shoot a narcotic.
Hit On – To ask for.
Hog – PCP.
Holding – See Dirty.
Holding – Having drugs in one's possession.
Hooked – Addicted.
Hooker – Hustler, a Prostitute.
Hop – Opium for smoking. Narcotics for injection or inhalation.
Hophead – Hype; a drug addict.
Hopped Up – Under the influence of Narcotics.
Horse – Heroin.
Hot Shot – Cyanide or other poison concealed in Narcotics to kill a troublesome addict.
Hump – To work.
Hustling – Activities involved in obtaining money to buy drugs.
Hype – Drug addict; Hophead.

I

Ibogaine – Derived from the roots, bark, stem, and leaves of an African shrub.
Ice – Cocaine.
Ice Cream Habit – See "Chipping."
Idiot Juice – Nutmeg and water mixed for intoxication, largely used in prisons.
Indian Hay – Marijuana.
Informer – Stool; an addict assisting police in arresting peddlers.
Iron Horse – A city jail. Most other underworld terms (Can, Joint, Band House, etc.) are also used by addicts.

J

"J" – A joint of Marijuana.
Jag – Under the influence of Amphetamines.
Jailhouse High – A high obtained from eating nutmeg.
Jeff – To be obsequious, especially Negroes in relation to Whites.
Jive (adj.) – Worthless.

Jive (n) – Marijuana.
Joint – A Marijuana cigarette. The prison.
Jolly Beans – Amphetamines.
Joy Juice – Chloral Hydrate.
Joy Pop – Use of Heroin in small amounts occasionally.
Joy Powder – Heroin.
Jugs – Injectible Amphetamines.
Juice – Alcohol.
Juice Head – An Alcoholic.
Junk – Narcotics, usually Heroin.
Junker – A Narcotic Addict.
Junkie – Narcotic Addict.

K

Key – One kilo of Marijuana.
Kick – Stop using Narcotics through complete withdrawal.
Kick Back – The addicts almost inevitable return to Narcotics after having kicked the habit.
Kick Cold – Treatment in which the addict is taken off drugs suddenly.
Kilo – A large amount of Narcotics from a pusher's point of view; technically 2.2 pounds. See Key.
Knockers – The testicles. A woman's breast.
Knock Out Drops – Chloral Hydrate.

L

LA Turnabouts – See Coast-to-Coast.
Lamb – The passive receptor in a homosexual relationship.
Lame – Square.
Laughing Grass – Marijuana.
Lay Dead – To do nothing.
Lemonade – See Flea Powder.
Lettuse – Money.
Lid – A small quantity of Marijuana, usually about one ounce.
Lid Proppers – Amphetamines.
Lipton Tea – See Mickey Finn.
Lit – Under the influence of drugs.
Lit up – Under the influence of drugs.
Load – See "Deck."
Loco Weed – Marijuana.

Long-tailed Rat – Stool Pigeon.

Louse – A Stool Pigeon. (Also Finger, Finger Gee, Longtailed Rat, Mouse, Rat).

LSD – Acid, sugar cubes, trips. Lysergic Acid Diethylamide. Big "D." Hawk.

Luminal – A Barbiturate.

M

"M" – Morphine.

Machine – See Harpoon.

MDA – Synthetic simulant and hallucinogen.

Made – Recognized for what you are.

Main Line – (n) The vein, usually in the crook of the elbow, into which the needle addict injects Narcotics.

Main Line – (v) To inject Narcotics directly into a vein.

Maintain – Keeping your head during a difficult situation.

Maintaining – Injecting a Narcotic directly into a vein.

Manicure – Marijuana with everything removed except the leaves.

Marijane – Marijuana.

Marijuana – Bhang, Charas, Ganja, Grass, Hash, Hashish, Hay, Hemp, Indian Hay, Jive, Laughing Grass, Loco Weed, Marijane, Pot, Railroad Weed, Reefer, Rope, Tea, Texas Tea, Weed.

McCoy – Medicinal drugs in contrast to bootleg drugs.

Medical Hype – A person who has become accidentally addicted during medical treatment for illness or disease; one who obtains bonafide drugs through doctors or hospitals.

Mellowing – The period of a crash when a person is on Speed.

MESC – Mescaline; hallucinogenic drug derived from the bottoms of the Peyote cactus plant native to Central America and Southwestern United States. (Also Peyote).

Meth – Methedrine.

Methadone – Dooly, Dolophine Amidone.

Mickey – Chloral Hydrate.

Mickey Finn or Mickey – Chloral Hydrate in a drink to knock out a victim. Also Euphemistically, Lipton Tea. A powerful physic such as croton oil, slipped into a whiskey to make the victim sick or to drive him away from a hangout.

Mike – A microgram.

Miss Emma – Morphine.

Mojo – Narcotics of any kind in a contraband trade; but usually Morphine, Heroin, or Cocaine.

Monkey – A drug habit involving physical dependence.
Monkey on my back – Early abstinence symptoms. A drug habit.
Morphine – Hard Stuff. "M," Miss Emma, Morpho, White Nurse, White Stuff, Unkie.
Morpho – Morphine.
Mother – An individual's drug peddler.
Mouse – A Stool Pigeon.
Mr. Twenty-Six – a needle (refers to the guage of the needle).

N

Nailed – To be arrested.
Narc or Narcos – The law; narcotic agent.
Needle Fiend – An addict who gets pleasure from playing with the needle by inserting an empty needle for the psychological effect.
Needle Freak – One who enjoys using the needle. See Needle Fiend.
Needle Habit – A habit which is satisfied by hypodermic injections.
Needle Park – To New York addicts, upper Broadway and Sherman Square.
Needle Yen – A desire for Narcotics taken hypodermically. A masochistic desire to mainline.
Nembies – Nembutal.
Nemmies – Nembutal.
Nickel – A $5 bag of Narcotics or Marijuana; also a five-year sentence.
Nickel Deck – Five-dollar package of Heroin.
Nimbie – Nembutal.
Nimbies – Nembutal (Pentobarbital).
Nimby – Nembutal (Pentobarbital).
Nod – To be sleepy from a dose of drugs.
Nut City – A mythical place in which anyone feigning insanity is said to live.

O

O. D. – An overdose of Narcotics.
Off – Off of drugs, not to be taking drugs at the present time.
Off Someone – To kill someone or to beat someone up.
On Ice – In jail. To lie low or go out of sight temporarily. Wanted by the law.
On the Nod – Sleep from Narcotics.
OP – Opium.
Opiates – Narcotics. Generally either Opium, Morphine, or Heroin.
Opium – OP.
Orange Owsley – See "Owsley Acid."

Orangies – Dexedrine (Dextroamphetamine, orange colored, heart-shaped tablets).
Out-of-it – Confused, disoriented, unknowing; also, an outside person who is not part of the drug culture.
Out There – Confused.
Overjolt – Overdose of Heroin.
Owsley's Acid – LSD (West Coast slang after the illegal manufacturer, Augustus Owsley Stanley, III).
Owsley's Blue Dot – See "Owsley's Acid."
O.Z. – One ounce of Marijuana.

P

Pack Heat – To carry a gun.
Pad – User's home; place where he shoots up.
Paid off in gold – Arrested by a Federal officer who flashes his gold badge.
Panic – Shortage of Narcotics on the market.
Paper – A legal prescription for drugs.
PCP – Angel dust. Peace Pill. Hog.
Peace Pill – PCP.
Peaches – Amphetamine Sulphate in rose-colored, heart-shaped tablets. (Also Roses, Hearts, Bennies, Orangies).
Peanuts – Barbiturates.
Peddler – A seller of Narcotics.
Pep Pills – Amphetamines. Also, Wake-ups, Eye Openers.
Pet – The police.
Peter – Chloral Hydrate
Petes – Chloral Hydrate.
Peyote – Mescaline.
P.G. – Paregoric.
Phat – Well put together.
Piece – One ounce of Heroin; a gun.
Pill Head – Addict on pills.
Pin – See Harpoon.
Pink Owsleys – See "Owsley's Acid."
Pinks – Seconal (Seconbarbital Sodium).
Pipe – An Opium smoker.
Plant – Stash-cache of Narcotics.
Pluck – Wine.
P.O. – A parole or probation officer.
P.O. – Paregoric.

Pot – Marijuana.
Pratt or Prat – A hip pocket.
Psilocybin or Psilocyn – Hallucinogenic drugs derived from certain mushrooms generally grown in Mexico.
Purple Hearts – A Barbiturate.
Purple Owsley – See "Owsley's Acid."
Pusher – Seller or dealer of drugs.
Put On – To deceive by design; to make fun of or to mislead someone.
Put the bee on – The act of begging Narcotics.
Put the croaker on the send – A "fit" or spasm staged by an addict to elicit sympathy.

Q

Queen – Male homosexual.
Quill – Matchbook cover used to inhale Narcotics. Powdered drug is placed in fold.

R

Rags – Clothes.
Railroad Weed – Marijuana of poor quality.
Rainbow Roll – An assortment of vari-colored barbiturates, popular among addicts on the West Coast.
Rainbows – Amobarbital Sodium combined with Secobarbital Sodium in red and blue capsules. Also, Red and Blues and Double Trouble.
Rap – Talk.
Rat – Stool Pigeon.
R.D. – A Red Devil.
Red and Blues – See Rainbows.
Red Devils – See Reds.
Reds – Seconal; Secobarbital Sodium.
Reefer – Marijuana cigarette.
Riff – Train of thought.
Right On – Affirmation of a truth; encouragement or support.
Rip Off – Seal or purchase of false Narcotics.
Roach – Butt of a Marijuana Cigarette.
Roach Clip – A device used to hold the butt of a Marijuana cigarette.
Rope – Marijuana. So called because when smoked it smells of burning hemp.
Roses – Benzedrine (Amphetamine Sulphate), rose-colored, heart-shaped tablets.

Rosy – Wine.
Run – Period of addiction.
Rush – The intense orgasm-like euphoria experienced immediately after injecting a drug. Also, Flash.

S

Sam – Federal Narcotic Agents.
Satch – A method of concealing or smuggling drugs into jails.
Satchel – A girl
Scag – Heroin.
Scat – Heroin.
Scene – Where something is happening.
Schmeck – Heroin.
School Boy – Codeine.
Scorch – To abuse someone verbally and very severely.
Score – To find a source of drugs.
Script – A prescription written by a physician to obtain drugs.
Script Writer – A sympathetic physician; someone who forges prescriptions.
Seccy – Seconal (Secobarbital Sodium).
Seconal – Sleeping pill; depressant, Pinks.
Send it home – To inject Narcotics intravenously.
Serpent – See Harpoon.
Sewer – The vein into which drugs are injected.
Sex Punk – A male homosexual.
Shakedown – To be arrested or held without charges in order to persuade the addict to supply information to police.
Shank – Knife.
Shit – Heroin.
Shoot – See Maintaining.
Shooting Gallery – Place where several addicts gather to shoot dope.
Shoot Up – See Mainlining.
Short – Car.
Short Go – A small or weak shot.
Shrink – A psychiatrist or psychologist.
Shucking – Wasting time.
Shy – To prepare a pill of Opium for smoking.
Silver – See Harpoon.
Silver Serpent – See Harpoon.
Sissy – A male homosexual.
Sitter – An individual who is sophisticated in the use of drugs, who will

oversee others who are on LSD to make sure they don't harm themselves.
Sixteenth Spoon – Sixteenth of an ounce of Heroin.
Skin – Cigarette paper used for a Marijuana cigarette.
Skin Popping – Injecting drugs under the skin.
Sleeping Pills – Barbiturates.
Smack – Heroin.
Smashed – High on drugs.
Sneaky Pete – Wine.
Sniff – To sniff Narcotics (usually Heroin, Cocaine, or Glue).
Snort – To sniff powdered Narcotics.
Snow – Cocaine.
Snowbird – A cocaine user.
Sound someone – To feel someone out.
Speed – Methamphetamine; any stimulant, especially, Amphetamines.
Speedball – A cocaine-heroin combination.
Speeder – A user of Methamphetamine.
Speed Freak – An excessive user of Methamphetamine.
Speeding – Using Methamphetamine.
Spike – See Harpoon.
Splach – Methamphetamine.
Split – To leave a place, sometimes in haste.
Spot Habit – See "Ice Cream Habit."
Square – Lame.
Stable – The community of girls who prostitute for one pimp.
Star Dust – Cocaine.
Stash – A place to hide drugs or money; generally a place well hidden but readily available.
Steam Boat – A tube such as an empty toilet tissue roll which is used to increase the amount of smoke from a Marijuana cigarette going into the lungs in order to increase the effectiveness of the cigarette.
Steam Roller – See Steam Boat.
Stick – A Marijuana cigarette.
Stir – Prison
Stoned – High on drugs.
STP – Hallucinogen; lasts for 72 hours.
Straight – An addict's feeling of well-being after taking drugs.
Strawberries – An LSD preparation.
Strung-out – Confused.
Stuff – Heroin.
Sugar – Narcotics, generally Heroin.
Sugar Cube – This is quite often a vehicle for LSD, a drop of LSD is absorbed

by the sugar cube before being taken.
Sunshine – An orange or yellow tablet of LSD reputedly to be of a very potent strength.
Swingman – A drug peddler.

T

T or T Man – A big man. A federal agent, especially a "narco."
Take a Trip – Using LSD.
Take Off – To smoke. To rob a place, especially of Narcotics.
Taste – Small quantity of Narcotics usually given as a reward or favor.
Tea – Marijuana.
Tea Man – A marijuana user.
Tecata – Heroin.
Ten-cent Pistol – Bag containing poison.
Texas Tea – Marijuana.
THC – Synthetic hallucinogen; produces same effect as Marijuana. Tetra Hydro Cannabinol. The active ingredients in Marijuana.
The Man – Policeman or Detective.
Ticket – A dose of LSD.
Tie Off – Stopping circulation in order for veins to rise.
Tight – Close.
Tinge – See Flash.
Tired – Old or worn out.
Tom Cat – See Harpoon.
Tooies – Tuinal capsules. See Double Trouble.
Tracks – Scars along the veins after many injections.
Trap – Prison.
Travel Agent – A person who sells LSD.
Trey – Three-dollar bag of Narcotics; generally Heroin.
Tripping – Taking a hallucinating drug.
Tripping Out – Same as Tripping.
Truck Drivers – Amphetamines.
Tuanol – Sleeping pill; depressant.
Tuinal – A barbiturate. Also called Rainbows or Double Trouble.
Turkey – Clod or square. A bag of non-narcotic powder sold as a regular bag.
Turn On – To be excited by; to get high on drugs.
TV Action – Euphoria from drugs.

U

Unkie – Morphine.

Uppers – Stimulants; Cocaine, Speed and Psychedelics.

V

Vegetable – A person who has lost all contact with reality due to drugs.
Very Outside – Extremely far out or weird.
Vet – A prison or jail physican.
Vines – Clothes.
Vipe – To smoke Marijuana.
Viper – A Marijuana smoker.

W

Wake Up – Morning shot.
Wake-ups – Amphetamines.
Wasted – Stoned or drunk.
Way Out – Incomprehensible. The best.
Weed – Marijuana.
Wheels – Car.
White Cross – A white tablet of Speed which is sectioned with a cross.
White Lady – Heroin.
White Nurse – A term used to cover Cocaine, Morphine or Heroin; but more often Morphine
White Owsley's – See Owsley's Acid.
Whites – Amphetamine Sulphate in round, white double-scored tablets.
White Stuff – "M," Hard Stuff, Morphine.
Wig – Head, hair.
Wig Out – To become psychotic as a result of Narcotics.
Wine – Grapes, Pluck, Rosy, Sneaky Pete.
Wired – Addicted on a Narcotic drug.
Works – Equipment for injection of drugs.

Y

Yellow Jackets – Nembutal, Barb, depressant. Phenobarbital Sodium in yellow capsule form.
Yellows – Nembutal.

Z

Zonked – Under the influence of Narcotics.

REFERENCES

Cull, J. G. and Hardy, R. E.: A study of language meaning (gender shaping) among deaf and hearing subjects. Journal of Perceptual and Motor Skills, 1973a, *36,* 98-99.

Cull, J. G. and Hardy, R. E.: Language meaning (gender shaping) among blind and sighted students. Journal of Psychology, 1973b, *83,* 333-334.

Hardy, R. E. and Cull, J. G.: Verbal dissimilarity among black and white subjects: a prime concern in counseling and communication. The Journal of Negro Education, 1972, XLII:1, 67-70.

INDEX

A

Alcoholic, 52, 155
Amphetamines, 19, 107, 109

B

Barbiturates, 46, 68, 100, 107
Barker, Art, 3, 7, 8
Barker, Shelly, 3
Berne, Eric, 12
Broward County Personnel Association, 8

C

Cocaine, 52, 97, 100, 143
Community Participation, 11
Cooperative Area Manpower Planning System (CAMPS), 9
Counseling, 87, 104, 147, 160
Cull, John G. (Mr. and Mrs.), v
Cull, J. G., 5, 9, 12

D

Daytop Village, 25
Detoxification, 4, 22, 31, 68, 81, 84, 100, 101, 139
Dismus House, 26, 27
Drug Abuse, 5, 7, 42, 52, 64, 72, 89, 100, 111, 158
Drug Addiction Specialist, 99
Drug Addicts, 23, 30, 59
Drug Therapy, 116

E

Encounter groups, 28
Ex-drugees, 9

G

Glue Sniffing, 155
Group Therapy, 5, 6, 8, 27, 28
Guidance, 87
Guided Group Interaction, 10, 11

H

Halfway House, 98, 104, 105, 106, 116, 140, 141, 144
Hallucinogenics, 48, 68, 69, 143
Hardy, Clifford E. (Mr. and Mrs.), v
Hardy, R. E., 5, 12
Hash, 17
Heroin, 16, 17, 21, 43, 46, 52, 60, 64, 65, 67, 68, 71, 75, 82, 96, 100, 103, 119, 125, 131, 139, 141, 147, 150, 158, 159, 162, 167, 171, 172
Heroin Addicts, 21

I

Individual Therapy, 27

J

Junkies, 21

L

LSD, 32, 33, 39, 52, 82, 90, 93, 95, 100, 101, 107, 109, 126, 131, 135, 158, 160

M

Marijuana, 16, 18, 21, 46, 52, 68, 75, 90, 96, 124, 131, 135, 142, 145, 155, 158, 160, 167, 171

Methadone, 4, 23, 44, 52, 54, 60, 64, 66, 70, 75, 76, 81, 84, 87, 100, 101, 124, 131, 146, 148, 159, 160

N

Narcotic paraphernalia, 22
Nembutals, 20, 146

O

"OD"ed, 25
Opium, 18

P

Paranoia, 90
"Pot", 17, 18, 20
Psychedelic Drugs, 109
Psychiatric Evaluation, 41, 50, 77, 103, 169
Psychiatric Therapy, 54
Psychiatric Ward, 22
Psychological Evaluation, 35, 38, 41, 42, 48, 54, 61, 64, 72, 77, 86, 91, 103, 108, 119, 123, 128, 132, 146, 162, 168, 172
Psychotherapy, 50, 51

R

Reality Groups, 28
Referrals, 11
Rehabilitation Counselors, 38, 46, 58, 66, 70, 88

S

Seconal, 82
SEED, 3, 4, 6, 7, 9, 10, 11, 12
Sensitivity Groups, 28
Serum Hepatitus, 23, 24, 52, 54, 68, 84, 121, 123, 148, 160, 164
Schizophrenia, 67, 68, 70, 104, 117, 155, 171
"Smack", 32, 33, 160
Social Worker, 58, 131, 132
"Speed", 39, 82, 90, 93, 107, 132, 148
"Straight", 5

T

Therapeutic Community, 25
Transactional Analysis, 10
Tuminals, 19

U

Urbanik, Richard, 12

V

Viet Nam, 17

W

Welfare, 59
Work Therapy, 27, 28